ENAMELLED IN FIRE

For the words of love are not written in water, but, as
Plutarch said:- " Enamelled in Fire"

In Memory of The Rev. Canon Robert Winnett, Ph.D., D.D.,
Friend, Mentor and Guide

HELEN FORSYTH

Printed and Published in 1994 by
Sutton Print Partners
60a Church Drive, Carrington, Nottingham. NG5 2BA
Telephone 0602 602348

ISBN 0-9523389-0-4

© 1994

ACKNOWLEDGEMENTS

The Editor acknowledges the following publications in which some of Helen Forsyth's poems were first printed.

The Writer's Review
The Hibbert Journal
This England
Tribune
Outposts
Without Adam (Anthology of Women Poets)
Homes and Gardens
The New Rambler
Quest (India)
Circulation (U.S.A.)
The National Guardian (Kenya)
Orbis
Isthmus
The Annals of The Royal College of Surgeons, England
The Literary Review
Rhyme Revival Anthology
The Contemporary Review
The Lichfield Mercury
Fresh Reflections on Samuel Johnson (U.S.A.)
The Nova Scotia Medical Journal (Canada)
Poetry Year Book for 1958
Sonnets for Shakespeare
Sennet
Reed (Spain)
A Burning Candle (Anthology of The Literary Review)
Proceedings of the Royal Society of Medicine

Her sonnets to John Keats and to Samuel Johnson are framed and on display in the Keats' Memorial Library, Hampstead, London, and The Johnson Room, Pembroke College, Oxford.

The fairy tales were right and they were wrong,
The Princess always found her perfect Prince,
And happy ever after was the song
We learnt as children and have wanted since.
A hedge of thorn was powerless to keep
The ardent bridegroom from the ardent bride,
A hundred years was not too long to sleep
For love triumphant would not be denied.
But life does not possess this magic charm,
And men and women lack a binding spell,
And likenesses so different feed alarm,
And each in isolation fathoms hell.
Rapunzel can't let down her lovely hair,
The ivory tower stays without a stair.

FOR CHEELIE

Edwin Rowse, a miner, was killed through the carelessness of an engine-driver, who was drunk at the time and let go the skip, which crashed to the bottom of the shaft. When the poor boy was brought up to the surface dying - he was almost cut in two by the crashed skip - he said these last words: "I've neither father nor mother to grieve for me, so it's all right."

Unknown philosopher of life and death
This is your marble monument. Your praise
A sonnet's words. Your asphodels its breath.
Your roses those that poetry conveys.
In this small space I write of such a one
As histories have honoured. One who spoke
The soul's inditement with his dying tongue,
His strength unbroken though his body broke.
A boy who found the rushing tides of pain
Were altered by the currents of his heart,
Who balanced death and found the value vain
When those he would not wound were spared the smart.
And with an equilibrium sublime,
Equated love for ever, and all time.

Tumescent hope, gone giddy with the spring,
Unspin yourself before you come to grief,
These careless blossoms do not mean a thing
Their beauty is no basis for belief
That life will be as lovely as they look,
Or love be simultaneous with the sun,
Their absolute fulfillment is no book
Where you can read the joy that is to come.
Identify with flowers if you must,
Admit the whirling tenderness of spring,
But realize in life you have to trust
To chance or what inconsequence may bring.
The flowers can be certain of their season,
But human hearts are subject to high treason.

"If it goes out, it must come back," they said,
"The sea is not so dominant as the moon,
The tide will turn with all its music spread
Before the one in rhythm with its tune.
Remember, Rome was not built in a day,
The bricks must bake, and then the bricks must cool,
And patience, that great virtue, will repay
The hesitating angel, not the fool."
And so I shut my passion in a cage,
And nailed my feeling to a wooden cross,
Impervious, however love might rage,
Intransigent, however pain might toss.
And Rome was built, but when the tide came strong
I found it brought the echo, not the song.

Love, that was once my own, has now become
Part of a pattern I no longer trace,
The thudding of my pulse involves a drum
That beats for more than one beloved face.
My vigil-sharpened vision sees the need
That forms the bitter nucleus of pain,
My burnt-forever fingers touch the seed
Divided from the tenderness of rain.
And love, in me betrayed, is now a part
Of continents of suffering everywhere,
The child's untutored grief has reached my heart
And unknown passions tremble in my prayer.
My separate love combines a million fears,
And when I weep, I shed the whole world's tears.

SHAKESPEARE

Shakespeare <u>is</u> immortal. He cannot escape
his crown and sceptre.

Reynor Barton

Your excellence has won a world's acclaim.
Your drama is rehearsed in many lands,
And April decks the glory of your name
With annual blossom from adoring hands.
Your sonnets are the loveliest we know.
Your plays reveal our natures to our eyes.
The full-force of your genius is a flow
Of words no other poet could devise.
We claim you as our Monarch, and we bring
The King's regalia to the vacant throne.
The heralds sound, the choirs start to sing
As you advance to take what is your own:
Sceptre and crown, and sovereignty still higher,
Immortal Laurel and Immortal Lyre!

"But did you not know, my darling dear, that the
poets lie?"

Samuel Johnson.

They do not mean to, but their heedless hearts,
So earnest and so ardent, magnify
The central truth from which their feeling starts
Until it forms a fretwork to the sky.
They do not mean to, but their eager eyes
See present and potential as the same,
And claim the joys their love can visualize
Forgetting life has loss as well as gain.
And yet their lie contains a truth that we
Unknowingly acknowledge every day,
For feelings are both extant and to-be,
Intangibles with which the mind can play.
Forgive the poets that they race ahead
To reach the joy before the tears are shed.

That August dawn of opalescent blue,
That overt orchestration of first cries,
Contained an agony I never knew
For ecstasy provisioned a disguise.
That later day with every cloud set high,
That thrilling unison of wind and sun,
Revealed no shadow I could reckon by
To plot the holocaust that was to come.
The love so certain of its perfect joy,
The unsuspected relevance of tears,
Became a passion nothing could destroy,
A power that would subjugate the years,
But how could early innocence suppose
That life would prove the laurel, not the rose?

I who withstood the sickening whine of planes
With their grim death,
Am now betrayed by tumult in the veins
And ardent breath.

I who was staunch when London's sky was fire
And bombers roared,
Am coward when the sharp blade of desire
Forms passion's sword.

I who endured the blood and toil of war,
The fear and flame,
Am vanquished when my heart repeats no more
Than just your name.

CHRIST.

Was the star
Bright as the pain
Of giving love
To men in vain?

Were the Kings
Reduced to three
To illustrate
The Trinity?

Was the flight
From blood in spate
The millstone of
Malignant fate?

Was the city
On the hill
The earthly one
You couldn't fill?

Were the pure
In heart to be
The neighbours of
Your constancy?

Were the tears
Upon your feet
Pardon for
The scourge's beat?

Was the kiss
Upon the cheek
Manifesto
Of the weak?

Was the cross
A tortured span
Of wood from God
And nails from man?

SAMUEL JOHNSON

"Dr. Johnson is an honour to mankind."

Rev.Martin M'Pherson

All great men are an honour to their land,
But you are more - an honour to mankind -
For you allowed your genius to expand
Until it reached a breadth few others find.
Your brilliant mind was governed by your heart
Your heart was governed by your brilliant mind,
They formed a dyad no event could part
And after death their glory was enshrined,
For Boswell wrote your Life and brought to view
The mercy that your judgement never lacked,
The primacy of virtue that was true
To every aspect of your every act,
The culminating goodness that became
Immortal as the letters of your name.

And the little foxes, darling,
That betray me when they bark,
Will the robin and the starling
Help me find them in the dark?

Will the branches break before me,
And the wind be at my side,
Will their passion still implore me
With a pain I can't divide?

Oh the little foxes, sweeting,
Will you hold them till they die
In a joy as swift and fleeting
As a comet in the sky?

This is the first time that the dusk has stayed
Night-filtered blue,
And not become a loveliness that frayed
My heart for you.

This is the first time that the winter trees
Are shapes apart,
And not a branching ecstasy that frees
You in my heart.

This is the first time that my mind can see
What I can't feel,
This is the counterpart of agony
As cold as steel.

I claim the idle beauty that we miss
The clouds we only see when in a plane,
The spectacle when sun and ether kiss
The ambience da Vinci sought in vain.
I claim the tops of forests and the snow
United to the lonely mountain height,
I claim the lofty winds that only blow
About the upper reaches of the night.
And then I claim the sympathies that bloom
To waste their sweetness on the desert air,
Affinities that never can assume
The dignity of love, and so despair.
I claim the unseen loveliness on high
And all the pensive passions that must die.

JOHN KEATS

When I behold, upon the night's starred face,
Huge cloudy symbols of a high romance,
The bias of your innocence and grace
Pervades my soul, and in a passioned trance
I hear the beating of a heart that heard
The nightingale releasing her refrain,
As ecstasy of beauty that deferred
The fear of death, and all the mounting pain
Of thoughts, full-ripened, that might never fill
The page bequeathed by Shakespeare's mighty hand,
Of love, lust-tightened, that would never spill
In unreflecting kisses, but would stand
Upon the primal, unrelenting shore
Where genius feels the ultimate implore.

THE EARLY DEATH OF MOZART

Whom the gods love die young, and their decree
Condemned the youthful Mozart while his head
Was filled with all the beauty that would be
His gift to life when life should find him dead.
But though he left us soon, he left us much
That time could not improve and cannot fade.
The Magic Flute gave music at his touch
And made Amphion's lyre feel afraid.
Such fountains of sheer sound, such flights of song,
Such genius, joy and harmony combined,
Have left a legacy that will belong
To each succeeding era of mankind.
The gods could not have loved him more than we,
But they had precept and priority.

Amphion had received a lyre from the god Hermes, on which he played with such
magic skill that the stones moved of their own accord and built the city of Thebes.

Between the fretted branches of the trees
The sun glows red,
An arabesque of sullen winter leaves
Around his head.

Beside the hedge the skeletons of stalks
Stand sere and brown,
An infamous predicament that mocks
Their summer crown.

From the damp earth there rises sharp and keen
The bracken's smell,
Nostalgic incense of another scene
I loved too well.

"The wounded normally fall in the direction of their wound"
Lucretius.

Lucretius says the wounds are war and love,
The desperate dagger or the deadly dart,
The brutal breach below, the bolt above,
Confusing the chiasmus of the heart.
The Epics made it clear that war brought pain,
And hate and fury under-satisfied,
But why should love produce a scarlet rain,
A rose so red needs no additional dyes!
But paradox confounds complexity
When wounded seeks the wounder in a fall,
For love and war have ceased to disagree
And demonstrate no difference at all.
But love restores its losses with such bliss
That kingdoms crash, and are not even missed.

For Wilfred Owen, M.C.

And each slow dusk a drawing-down of blinds.
Anthem for Doomed Youth.
Wilfred Owen

And each slow dusk a drawing-down of blinds.
Perhaps for other soldiers, not for you,
For you have left us poetry that shines
Through every shade that Time can fasten to.
And though you mourned for others, we rejoice
That Death can not divide us from your mind,
That we can share the pity and the choice
Of wilder beauty than our lives can find.
But sorrow is terrestrial! You belong
On that high plateau where great poets go,
You have enriched Parnassus with your song
And taught the flowers of tenderness to grow.
And on those heights where night can never fall,
You prove the reason why the clay grew tall.

ON RICHARD READING HIS ENCYCLOPAEDIA

With solemn mouth and meditative eyes,
Your burnished head is bent above your book,
And gentle as a dove within you lies
The innocence concurrent with your look.

The printed image leaps to your swift mind,
And you become the heir of many lands,
But where, within the covers, could I find
The heritage implicit in your hands?

Oh, lovely child involved in deep surmise,
No words contain the joy you bring to me,
For even the orchards found in Paradise
Have no such apple hanging on the tree.

The trees are brown again, and Autumn fades
The bright green sonnet of my summer dream,
The words like roses and the secret glades
Of passion waiting for our love's extreme
Have altered now, and I can hardly trace,
In falling leaf and branches nearly bare,
The rhythm and the structure of your face,
The measurement in music that I care.
The sun is mellow, and his gentle rays
Can scarcely spread the petals of a flower,
But I am left with suffering that stays
Extended to our pleasure's fullest hour,
For Autumn with its wood-smoke and its mist
Has not concealed the moment when we kissed.

And shall we meet at last, my tireless one,
You who have moved towards me since my birth,
Beneath the blackened night and blinding sun,
With patient feet traversing half the earth?
And shall we speak in silence, though we know
The lark less lyric than our thoughts of love,
Yet be content to let the image go
And only claim the presence of the dove?
And shall we feel a wonder that explores
The evanescent patterns of the past,
A penetrating passion that ignores
Ephemerals too fugitive to last,
And in complete fulfillment of the dream
Shall we continue what has never been?

To have, but not to hold, and yet to be
Receptive to a passion that is there.
To see, yet not to say, what sympathy
Brings us together in a sweet despair.
To feel, but not declare, the secret flame
That confiscates the centre of my heart,
To re-possess what I can never claim
And find the sweetness stronger than the smart,
Is but half-hearted pleasure, and I long
For the full circle of entirety.
I want the singer and I want the song
And every tacit promise offered me.
I want it all, the man, the mind, the heart,
And cannot be content with one small part.

SAMUEL JOHNSON

Myrtles are insufficient for your story,
And laurels lack the tenderness to show
Beneath the granite-grandeur of your glory
The frailest rose of love was safe to grow.
Fanfares, indeed, are fitting for your fame,
But trumpets, rich and regal though they be,
Have not the gentleness that can proclaim
Compassion with each earthly misery.
Oh, great, good, man, England will never find
Another genius she would rather show,
For intellect and virtue thus combined
Exceeds the utmost excellence we know,
And proves that at his highest man might be
The greatest triumph of eternity.

PAUL HAMILTON WOOD

You were a doctor whom the whole world sought,
Yours was the dictum, verdict, final word,
Yours was a mind its own pre-eminence taught,
Yours was a focus trials never blurred.
Yours was a questing brilliance that threw light
On the cross-currents of the body's tide,
Yours was a fame whose vision could incite
Surgeons to place their daring at your side.
Yours was a gift that could not be denied,
Though dedication took increasing toll
Until your heart, so passionately tried,
Could not support your spirit's valiant role.
But we, who saw your greatness pay such price,
Have watched the ultimate in sacrifice.

VILLANELLE

To think one thought a hundred, hundred ways
And tease the questing sequence of the mind
To fill the loveless vacuum of the days.

To penetrate the enigmatic maze
And prove the swift synapses were designed
To think one thought a hundred, hundred ways.

To dream of love with all the sweet delays
That memory's minutiae can find
To fill the loveless vacuum of the days,

And with concurrent logical assays
To demonstrate no unity can bind
To think one thought a hundred, hundred ways,

Are scintillating, cerebral displays
That cannot cheat a God already blind
To fill the loveless vacuum of the days.

But tremble, lest he seek Apollo's rays
And bring to life the senses you resigned
To think one thought a hundred, hundred ways
To fill the loveless vacuum of the days.

Leaves have never looked so bright as this,
So brilliant, buoyant, beautiful and brash,
For yellow, bronze and brown unite and kiss
And red and green commingle as they clash.
Leaves have never seemed so glad and gay,
So rich in beauty, though so poor in time,
Another month will whirl them all away,
And yet the wind is guiltless of this crime.
This theft is part of nature's cunning plan
To limit loveliness unto desire,
So well she knows the fickle heart of man,
Too soon complacent and so quick to tire.
And so she wafts away her lovely leaves
Lest if they linger they should cease to please.

Momus, God of Censure, said man should have a window in his breast, to enable one to look into his secret thoughts.

Momus desired a window in the breast
So all could see if thought and act agreed,
To ascertain if feelings were possessed
Of hidden, undermining calumnies.
Momus desired a double-check to find
The final truth of what a man might say,
The ultimate no sophistry could wind
According to a calculated way.
But what if the seclusion only hides
The dearness of a love that can't be told?
The depth-beneath-the-depth that still abides
However sweet the words, however bold!
I would not shun a window of display
To let you read what words can never say.

I feel the song with such a wild delight
A feral madness rises in my veins,
And I am drowned in the swift fountain's flight
And feel my body fall in golden rains;
In rains of love that quench the fire of death
And grow immortal flowers in the heart,
In ecstasy, that gives undying breath
To words that tear the very soul apart.
Oh efflorescence of the body's core,
Oh bursting star of passionate delight,
Oh tideless sea against the perfect shore,
Oh consummation of the day and night.
The music beats in breast and blood and bone,
Eternal rhapsody with notes of stone.

How could I think of anything but you,
Caught, as I was, in such a web of charm
That ever-widening thraldom only drew
Me further from the signposts of alarm?
How could I see the path was set with flint,
When such a mist of promise veiled my eyes
It seemed a highway petalled without stint
That opened with a fanfare of birds' cries?
And even now I cannot bear to see
The fragile trestles of my towering joy,
I thought them pillars that eternity
Would need its utmost power to destroy;
But life can break the heart as well as death,
And love is at the mercy of a breath.

Wrong is not made right by time,
Though months may moss the lancing thorn,
However high the rose may climb
The wounded palm will still be torn.

Distance does not alter facts,
Nor a new town remove the old
Where love was played in all its acts
And passion was a cloth-of-gold.

What is, exists, and cannot be
Denied, because a different air
Has blown the leaves of memory
From branches so intensely fair.

Fold up the petal
Roll back the leaf,
If it didn't happen
We can't feel grief.

Cancel the memory
Unkiss the hand,
Be like the ostrich
Safe in the sand.

Add up our feelings
Rub out the score,
Then we should be
As we were before.

Bright glow the ashes
Where the bird rose,
But we have forgotten
What our heart knows.

Today I saw the innocence of pain,
The questing look that quilts a blinded face
The absence of reaction and the strain
Of walking paths that vision cannot trace.
I saw the blossom of the rose exchanged
For Lenten lilies, and the straitened line
Of lips much meant for laughter rearranged
In sad acceptance of a cruel design.
And suddenly the hardship that I bore,
The tyranny of fierce creative fire,
Became a torment that I could ignore
A difference I even could desire.
Today I saw the innocence of pain.
I shall not need the lesson taught again.

SAMUEL JOHNSON

He fought his weaknesses and found his strength,
He triumphed in his wit and balanced prose.
He smiled when Boswell questioned him at length
On whims and fads and likes and loves and foes.
He gave sane judgements, and he settled words,
He rescued Shakespeare from despoiling hands,
His Pembroke was a nest of singing birds,
His London was the centre of all lands.
He worshipped Christ with love beyond belief,
He reckoned values for the works of men.
His pity pleaded for the whore and thief,
He sifted blame, and then employed his pen
To leave us truths no fallacy can part,
That rise like angels in the human heart.

FOR THE MOTHER OF LESLEY ANN DOWNEY

No word can ease this grief, no touch avail
To soften the sheer sorrow that you know,
The unremitting malice of this tale
Obliterates all other source of woe.
Your anguish proves faith faithless, for no prayer
Can bring a melting peace from lenient skies,
While you recall the movement of her hair,
The unimpeded beauty of her eyes.
So nothing one can say or one can do
Can mitigate the grinding force of pain,
The savage picture that the sadists drew,
The image that is blazing in your brain.
But when this searing hate burns to a close,
Your love will prove commensurate with the rose.

The days have stretched their arms to clasp the spring,
And twilight lengthens in a saffron light
Behind bare branches that the sun will bring
To buds and birds and blossoms of delight.
The rusted willow bends above the pond
And dreams demurely of the grey and green
Eternal to her branches by the bond
She holds with every summer that has been.
And I, alone, am promiseless and bear
No tightly-budded hope that could expand
Into a wreath of roses for my hair,
Into a sheaf of corn for my hand.
Oh lovely trees secure in nature's sun,
Pity the buds that die for lack of one.

Oh love, what made you send this sudden storm!
Was summer over-precious that you drew
A barrier of clouds designed to form
Exclusion from the ambience we knew?
Oh love, what made you meet me clothed in mail,
With vizor tightly fastened and your sword
So menacing and ready, should I fail
In absolute obedience to my lord.
I was your subject, darling, not your foe,
I knew my standing and our twin delight
Was captured where my ecstasy could grow
Without impairment of your sovereign right.
Oh cruel king to offer me a rose,
And then to fill its petals with such snows.

Release me from your love's unfailing band,
The time has come to set my heart quite free,
To cut the silver ribbon that your hand
Once bound so tight and tied so tenderly.
Four years have wound their length around that band,
Four years like seasons - Autumn, Winter Spring,
But Summer blooms for you in a far land,
And leaves me flowerless, and suffering.
You were incomparable - I shall not find
Resemblance of you anywhere I go,
Life holds no counterfeit to cheat my mind
To hide this rose beneath a cloud of snow.
The falcon falling on the helpless dove
Is not more catastrophic than my love.

DR. DANIEL BLOOMFIELD

America is not your heritage,
It is your home and so its hold is strong,
But it is scribbled notes upon a page
Beside the ancient beauty of your song.
America is but your place of birth,
An accident of river and of plain,
The evanescent pattern of her earth
Can't mar the fixed mosaic of your name.
You walk her ways and gratitude demands
You answer any favour she may ask,
But though you give the blessing of your hands
Stay faithful to your more important task:
To keep alive the feeling of the race
That made man's one unchanging perfect face.

No dog can drag the mandrake of this lie
Out of the soil of truth I thought we shared.
It rots the rose and makes the lilies die,
And strips the roots of love and leaves them bared.
It blights what was the wheat of summer days,
And drains the lovely colour from the leaves
Of our remembered autumns, till the blaze
Of what we felt becomes a flame that grieves.
This rope of sand that I thought hoops of steel,
This flowering love that hid a waste of lies,
This festival of all the flesh could feel,
This sin that was so perfectly disguised,
Have now combined to abrogate the past
And cancel moments that were meant to last.

ON WATCHING A HEART OPERATION

This is the heart, but not as poets dreamed it,
Rich fountain of a thousand different flows,
This is the heart as Harvey's genius schemed it,
Four-chambered pump with petals like a rose.
This is the heart, but not as poets see it,
Insurgent centre of tumultous joy,
This is the heart as surgeons' scalpels free it
And scientific stratagems employ.
This is the heart torn from its tender sac,
Denied its pulses, cheated of its blood,
Until the moment, rhythm given back,
It manages its own triumphant flood.
And looking in the theatre I view
A love as keen as any Venus knew.

S A M U E L   J O H N S O N
Died 1784.

We meet this year in memory of your death,
In reverence, in tribute and the joy
That your past words are warm with present breath,
That death can neither alter nor alloy
The magnitude of manhood that still lives
In Boswell's <u>Life</u>, in essays and in deeds.
The magnitude of manhood that still gives
The Christian answer to our human needs.
We pause before two centuries of time,
Two centuries when any questing mind
Could read your thoughts, the legacy sublime
That genius wed to virtue left mankind.
Two hundred years have but increased the fame
Of your illustrious and beloved name.

Is love an accident, and hate the rule,
Is mercy a mutation of the mind
And universal suffering a school
Where tenderness plays truant for mankind?
Is Lear the symbol of our passion's scope,
Is pain the parallel in every plan?
A feather's flutter breaks the hangman's rope,
Insanity secures a moment's span.
Yet love is stronger than its iron pains,
And tears can't drown it though a million weep,
Intangible, yet trenchant, it remains
Above the barriers the flesh must keep.
For love can not be coffined with its doom,
But rises regnant from the deepest tomb.

Cages are built with silences or words,
But we built ours with both, because we knew
That either might give way, and then the birds
Of all we felt would collocate in view.
Cages restrain. Alas, they don't conceal
The precious prisoners behind their bars:
We let our words and silences reveal
How perilously beautiful were ours.
Was it your fault or mine, this recognition?
If stars do not design what is to be,
We both must share the blame and the contrition
For images denied their liberty.
Cages restrain. Alas, they also fail!
We saw the tree. We heard the nightingale.

I seek the aftermath of pain,
The anaesthetic interval,
When the burning thought in the beating brain
Is suddenly ephemeral:
When the heart is numb and the pulse is slow
And the mind is blocked and can resist
The thrust and parry, feint and blow
Of love the cruel antagonist;
Of Love the foe who refuses peace,
But battles on in the heart's red lair,
Insatiate, his lust increased
By every tremor, every tear.
I seek the aftermath of pain,
Or the renaissance of the slain.

Gaze not on swans! Their beauty is too swift
And takes us prisoner ere we can turn
And leave a loveliness that seems to drift
In faultless feathers. It can also burn!
Gaze not on swans! Their power is too pure,
Their grace too gorgeous, and their mighty wings
Can fold us in a circle that is sure
Of all the melting harmonies it brings.
Gaze not on swans if you would guard your heart
From magnitudes and marvels that contain
Imperatives so absolute they start
Exultance that is dangerous as flame!
Gaze not on swans unless your soul can bear
A beauty that could kindle its despair.

I am alone again and now must turn
To find a lesser truth to comfort me,
Must unremember verities that burn
And doubt convicton's authenticity.
Must question moments and the written word,
And chide myself for finding in your eyes
The lovely mastery that Eve conferred
On Adam for the loss of Paradise.
And so I seek a minor honesty
Safe from the major facts I thought I knew,
Until you taught me that fidelity
Was relative, not absolute or true.
But let us both acknowlege 'till we die
That truth was co-existent with the lie.

Are these my tears, or does the wind hold rain?
I hope they are not mine, for I had thought
That now I was intrinsicate with pain
All passion's trembling diamonds had been bought.
Is this my hurt, or does the night-bird cry?
I hope it is not mine, for then my pride
Closed in the cruellest armour fear could buy
Would faint to feel love's arrow in my side.
Is this my grief, or do I but reflect
The bitter-balance of a natural plan,
The thorn that makes the roses circumspect,
The tree that made an animal of man.
Is this the rain, the bird, the rose, the tree,
Confederate with nature, or with me?

Darling, what shall I do
With words I have not said?
Swift as a flight of birds
They circle in my head,
And though when I'm asleep
They fold their wings to rest,
With the first waking thought
They sweep across my breast.

Darling, what shall I do
With wayward tenderness?
It flows into my hands
Impatient to caress,
But all I touch is air,
And all that I can feel
Is the remembered flesh,
Alluring and unreal.

Darling, what shall I do
With love that won't regress,
Words I care to say,
Unanswered tenderness?
Is your hope so high,
Your heart so full of ease,
There are not moments when
You have not need of these?

The ribbons of hope
Have caught in your doubt,
They're braided severely
And twisted about,
And you have discarded
The passionate red,
And chosen a fatal
Crimson instead.

The colours are faded
The fabric is torn,
The lustre of promise
Is dull and forlorn,
And now they are altered,
You send them to me,
Fastened with gold
As a last cruelty.

The blossom broke before it reached the bough,
Fragility was inherent in the bud,
No passion of the sun could show it how
To bring its petals safely into flood.
Belief was simultaneous with the lark,
It rose as freely and it rose as true,
It cleaved the clinging curtains of the dark
And perished in the unexpected blue.
Love was a pattern love could never change,
The shuttle could not weave against the weft,
No matter how the colours were arranged
The reasserting motif was still left.
The fault was in the flesh and in the star
That placed the heavens higher than they are.

This sonnet is for you, my hidden lark,
My bird of Paradise, my lovely swan,
My nightingale that's sobbing in the dark,
My bluebird that is singing to the dawn.
This sonnet is for you, my hidden rose,
My fairest fair that nothing can conceal.
Triumphantly, your petals still enclose
The beating heart no other love could steal.
This sonnet is for you, it does not borrow
A present instance to repeat the past,
This sonnet is my joy's extremest sorrow
The proof exemplary that love can last.
This sonnet seeks you down a dale of years
With birds and roses, ecstasy and tears.

What we have now, contains what went before
As circles on the surface of a pond
Retain the vortex, though they still explore
The undivulged, contiguous beyond.
What we have learnt has now become a part
Of the expanding callipers we need
To plot the new circumference of the heart
And trace diameters we supersede.
But is this scope for us, or must we keep
Our fresh horizons for another map,
And draw the present precipice so steep
That love's geography becomes a trap?
If this is so, whatever plan we try
Is charted on the blue-print of a lie.

Another rose to see, but not to pick.
To touch, but not to take, although the glow
Of rosy petals yields a perfume thick
With all the sweetness I most want to know.
Another rose that nods its head to me
And spills across my fence, until I feel
The boundary a false security
Beside an incandescence that is real.
Oh why did fate and summer send a rose
To tempt and tease by showing what could be?
Have they no knowledge of a need that grows
Until it aches to answer such a plea?
Why should I bar my heart against this bloom
And long for life while I erect a tomb?

Is this what life leaves us after the years,
Hearts that are anguished, eyes without tears,
Hope that is doubtful, pain that is set,
Minds that remember what they should forget?
Is this what life leaves us as it moves on,
Grief that is over, love that is gone,
Hands that are lonely, lips that are tight,
Trust that has darkened until it is night?
Oh, let life engender a rose that is true,
Fragrant and glowing and gleaming with dew,
Open and ardent with nothing to hide,
Aware of its power and proud of its pride,
Rife with a beauty no winter can break
And set in a garden no soul can forsake.

This truth was always waiting for your mind,
But deeper truths were waiting for your heart,
What forced intention made you fail to find
That one contained the other from the start?
The thorn could not be seen, but it was there
Cocooned within the fibres of the past,
How could your probing fingers prise it bare
And not reveal a rose compelled to last?
Yours was a strength I had not met before,
Implacable as tempests when they blow
Reluctant waves to crash upon the shore
And make foam-flowers of unfathomed woe.
You could not part the passion from the pain
Unless the rose was fashioned in your name.

This miracle of joy that I must hide,
This wonder that you didn't know you gave,
This magic Pegasus I may not ride,
This largesse I can't spend, and so must save.
This zephyr of enchantment that could blow
My heart towards the mystery of you,
This burning rose beneath a veil of snow
With petals that your passion could renew.
This meeting that will pass, but which I hold
To span the coming stretch of dreary days,
Your Midas-gift that makes each moment gold,
Your voice that sang an anthem in your praise,
Are miracles of joy that will remain
Though separation lengthens into pain.

Death would never leave us ghosts like these
That still might come to life if they should meet
Without the cruel necessity to please
Or fear's swift sandals fastened to their feet.
For death does more than stop the ears and eyes,
It seals the deep embrasure of the mind,
No sudden swerves of memory can surprise
Mnemonics of a love we cannot find.
But your decree has beggared life and death
So neither can enrich the other's need,
The agony of life finds ample breath
And death, enslaved, has left remembrance freed.
If love can not restore me to your heart,
Kill me outright and let oblivion start.

Thoughts of a Driver who has Killed
a Woman on a Zebra Crossing.

This undreamed of moment should not be,
It has its roots in some unthinking past
That selfishly became the tragedy
That now confronts me, silently aghast.

The woman lying dead upon the road
Was killed by me, and by the moment when
My heart refused the chafing of the load
We bear each other in the name of men.

It is too late for pity and too soon
For full contrition, but a flying pain
Has pinned her stillness, lying in the gloom,
Across the waiting fineness of my brain.

You met me with the broad brow of a god,
Your eyes serene and wide as open flowers,
And though you spoke of science, I could nod
To Adonais, in his burning bowers.
You told me how the world could be confined
Within the slight circumference of a cup,
While Adonais, lovely head inclined,
Received my heart and burnt its vapour up.
And so you stay two people: one who traced
The fission-fusion of the dread explosion;
The other a bright god who gladly faced
The fiercer fire of the heart's corrosion.
But knowledge of you both at once discloses
A scientist with kisses like blurred roses.

The grey November day is like a stone
Heavy and dull, and yet the silent mist
Is phantomed with a hope so like my own
The strong intangibles of love persist.
Against the back-cloth of the day I weave
An idyll as ephemeral as fact,
With iridescent flowers to relieve
The ruthlessness your passion never lacked.
But like this winter day, I lead to spring,
To summer's fullness and to autumn's fruit,
While your supposed preponderence can bring
No efflorescence from its coward root.
And when new moons shall bring new flowers to me,
Your fear will prove its fearful enmity.

Pain is now fixed forever,
You set its limit when
You used the sword to sever
What love has joined again.

And so, apart-together,
In fierce anomaly,
You force my bliss to feather
The wings of agony.

FOR SHAKESPEARE OF THE SONNETS

"From me far off, with others all too near"
Did Shakespeare know the torment of that line?
Could his rich love be fastened to such fear?
Could his sweet favour suffer such decline?
"What potions have I drunk of Siren tears."
Did Shakespeare weep, and did he weep alone?
What love could be impervious to his fears?
What heart could beat indifferent to his own?
"Why didst thou promise such a beauteous day?"
But oh, my love, who could have promised less?
Faced with the passion that your words convey
A phoenix would set fire to its nest,
And if it perished in the lovely flame,
Its frailty, not its feeling, was to blame.

We can believe the thorns, but the rose
Seems unsubstantial, though its petals press
Against our mouth until our body knows
The fearful rapture of the first caress
That shattered Eden to rebuild the world
Superior to serpents, and to keep,
As apple-seed within his mother curled,
A pledge of passion eloquently deep.
We can believe the feeling, but the fact
Is unfamiliar to our inmost eye,
Reflections in a mirror that is backed
With silver splinters sharper than a cry.
We have had proof of thorns, but the rose,
Is evanescent when our fingers close.

Beset by galaxies, astray with stars,
Caught in the endless orbit of the spheres,
A microcosm that no finite bars,
A mote removed from love, restrained from tears.
Bathed in the beauty of the Milky Way,
Translucent as the lovely Pleiades,
And glittering with the sun's most recent ray,
Why is my human heart so hard to please?
Because this is forever in cruel calm,
With feeling futile as eternity,
This is the god indifferent to the psalm,
This is the moon oblivious of the sea.
Oh, won't some mystic meteor expose
The infinite that lies within a rose?

HORATIO NELSON

"But if it be a sin to covet honour,
I am the most offending soul alive."

Shakespeare

This quotation was frequently used by Nelson in his letters.
Nelson is buried in St. Paul's Cathedral.

High in Trafalgar Square his statue stands,
A slender figure thrust against the sky,
Honoured by us and those of other lands,
A man of courage, lacking arm and eye.
A man of courage of a special kind
Both physical and moral, but much more,
For love of England actively combined
In every battle to defend her shore.
A man of pulsing greatness, one whose name
Inspired duty by its very sound:
Whose business was with honour, not with fame,
Whose grave lies in his country's hallowed ground.
A man designed for glory, one who knew
That Shakespeare's words proclaimed what he would do!

FOR ROSEMARY

Yours is the final truth. No past can take
The present rainbow glowing in your sky.
Those trembling colours are your own heart's ache,
The Covenant no passion can deny.
Yours is the final love. No former pain
Can dim the roses gathered by your hand.
Those crimson petals are your own heart's stain,
The scarlet Christ was born to understand.
But all is over.   Love and Truth have come
Two weary pilgrims knocking on your door.
Their feet are pierced, their lips are cold and numb,
Yet with a holy pity they implore:
"Oh let us change the water into wine,
For suffering has made your thirst divine."

SONNET FOR THE MUSIC - MAKER

Of what were you afraid? That I should fail
To render unto Caesar what was due?
Or did you think my spirit could not scale
The steep Olympian heights that reach to you?
Then learn that you were wrong, that I possess
Fidelity that puts your own to shame,
For Distance found she could not make it less,
And Absence found she deified your name.
And further know, that not a single note
Of that extravagant, triumphant score,
That June-impassioned music that you wrote
But echoes in my heart for evermore.
I challenge you find a gauge to prove
That I have ever faltered in my love.

This short reprieve that leaves another day
When I may dream the rose is meant for me,
This sweet hiatus when my thoughts can play
With all the dear delights of sophistry.
This precious respite when I do not know
If I am right or wrong or what will be,
This ecstasy of knowledge that can slow,
The force of longing's bitter energy.
This lovely instant when I dare to hope,
This peacock moment with its spreading tail,
This interval when innocence has scope,
This counterpoise in life's uneven scale,
Has harboured me behind love's golden bars,
And decked me with a diadem of stars.

I think you gave me more than I first knew
When hope, retracted, filled my world with pain,
For though the love that blossomed never grew,
Its petals and its purity remain.
Your lips were touch made perfect and the song
I waited with such eagerness to hear
Was left involved in silence to prolong
The delicate retention in my ear.
I wanted further music and the flow
Of rhapsody in harmony with sound,
I wanted swift crescendos and the slow
Andante till the ecstasy was found.
But you within the tenure of a kiss
Revealed the actual-absolute of bliss.

The clove carnation in your blood is mine.
The other flowers wait a new love's start,
But you will find that always the design
Of fretted petals brings you to my heart.
The deepest music in your mind is mine.
The lighter scores are for a passing voice,
But in the symphony we so combine
That we remain each other's final choice.
Squander your roses with a careless hand,
Scatter the lovely petals of your May,
I am the flower you most understand,
I am the music you most long to play.
I am the clove carnation in your blood,
I am the essence of your soul in flood.

"Somewhere," she cried, "there must be blossom blowing."
Robert Graves.

Somewhere, she cried, there must be blossom blowing,
Perpetual winter was not Nature's plan,
Somewhere the buds of love must still be growing
And waiting for the garnering of man.
Somewhere, she cried, there must be fountains flowing,
Eternal ice was never meant to be,
Somewhere the silver water must be showing
Reflections of love's full complicity.
Somewhere, she cried, there must be Fates that harken
To lovers joined in divided ways,
Somewhere there must be skies that seldom darken
And woods where love can sing its roundelays.
Somewhere there must be sanctuary for bliss
And blossom blessing lovers as they kiss.

FOR ANTHONY GREY

Anthony Grey, Reuter's correspondent in Peking, was imprisoned for
777 days in solitary confinement in a darkened cell daubed with
Chinese characters.

On his release he was awarded the O.B.E.

You were not quite alone. Our spirit flew
Across the separation to your cell,
Our ever-present absence could construe
The grammar of your hieroglyphic hell.
You did not pace alone. Beneath the arch
Of England's sky of high supernal blue,
We felt the devastation of the march
Within the hidden room we never knew.
Yet day by dragging day you still sustained
The dignity of sanity and sense,
Incarceration lacked the force to change
The pattern of a courage so intense.
And as you leave to live your life apart
Our pride is iridescent as your heart.

Send me no lavender to store my grief
Neat as a sheet
Sweet-folded in the cupboard of my mind:
Immoderate roses could not bring relief
To this defeat
Or grace the victory you leave behind.

Send me no chiselled phrases to revoke
The wordless joy
Immediate to the language of your hand:
Though you retract each syllable you spoke
It won't destroy
The tongue-implicit ecstasy we spanned.

White tangents from the bough the pear tree sends
Her faultless blossom latticed with black bark,
And with slow ravishment the bluebell bends
Her petals round the axis of my heart.
With pennants of pale green the willow greets
The upstroke of the reassuring wind,
Most tenderly, the apple tree entreats
Forgiveness for the daring one who sinned;
But you, the central figure of my spring,
Stand obdurate, despite this lovely frame,
With cruel closed mouth no burgeoning can bring
To open to the cadence of my name.
Oh let the winter of your silence break
Into the spring of speech for beauty's sake.

I suffer the ferocity of love,
The fierce assault that makes the senses swoon,
The brutal bolt, the lightning from above
That cleaves the healing darkness into noon.
Relentless love with love's relentless skill
Allows no shadow, gives my pain no rest,
But bares the trembling mystery until
I find my heart is beating in your breast.
Bereft by love I watch my bastions fall,
My citadel becomes a cloud of clay,
I've no defence both wide enough and tall,
To shield me from this harsh expanding day.
How long can I endure this ruthless plight
Destroyed by day and yet denied the night?

The deaths we do not die remain as scars
Contracting the fair tissue of our hope,
And night becomes a blackness without stars,
And day becomes a freedom without scope.
The deaths that we outlive do not supply
Immunity to passion or to pain,
For sorrow lacks the strength to fortify,
And resignation ransoms love in vain.
So life proceeds uncertain of belief,
And love is always suspect, never sound,
And trust untrusting terminates in grief,
In anguish both afflictive and profound.
And life that should be sweet and swift of breath
Is robbed of every rose, save that of death.

I die of thirst beside the fountain's edge,
My eyes perceive what I can never claim,
But perilous with passion is the pledge
My blood repeats in homage to your name.
I hunger by the fruits of Paradise,
And long to taste what I must never know,
Although my yielding senses realize
Such visions only make my torment grow.
And yet I think the coldest hermit's cell
Could scarce reduce so vehement a fire,
The fiercest conflagration found in Hell
Would flicker in the face of such desire.
Yet I restrain a force I could not measure
For fear it should occasion your displeasure.

The high blue winds of March have blown my heart
Into the waiting branches of your mind,
And I am disenfranchised by an art
Most artless where it most has been designed.
For though each twig can claim its parent bough,
And every leaf identify its stem,
There is no plan to show your prisoner how
She can escape the rising sap of them.
And such a sap must succour many flowers,
Break with bright blossom through the binding bark,
Substantiate the sempiternal powers,
The coronal coeval with the dark.
Oh wanton winds! Oh more than lovely tree,
That holds me fast when most it sets me free!

For Dr. Towers, on the Death of his Son.

This spring won't hold the brightest flower you knew,
Though white and gold and purple stain the grass,
The clearest sky won't equal the lost blue
Of matchless eyes no heaven could surpass.
No morning madrigal to greet the day
Will catch the cadence of one childish voice
That love made music. Nor can swans delay
The whiter wings that robbed you of your choice.
But when full summer burns the buds of spring
And offers you its deepest, reddest rose,
May the dark beauty of such petals bring
Peace to a wound that time can never close;
May summer's triumph tear your pain apart,
And loveliness restore him to your heart.

Must every petal perish at my touch,
And every flower fade within my hand?
The short span of a summer is not much
To hope the rose will last and not expand
Into a passioned perfume that evokes
A beauty bitter as the barren dust,
A lethal loveliness that only chokes
The breath of hope, the breathlessness of trust.
Does nothing last until it is fulfilled
And breaks in fruit and comes to leaf again?
Have seasons changed? Is summer never thrilled,
Or autumn raptured through the mists of pain?
Oh let this blossom last that I may wear
A garland round my heart, and in my hair.

This April love is very hard to bear,
Its blossoms fragile and its showers cold,
I cannot trust a sun, however fair,
Who disappears in winter's sullen fold;
And though a sudden burst of song may take
My heart's crescendo in its feathered throat,
It only needs a sudden chill to make
The lyric finish on a dying note.
For every sweet seems balanced with a sour,
And every warmth the twin of killing frost,
The barren earth is ruptured by a flower,
And then the flower itself is tempest-tossed.
The compass is bewitched that can proclaim
The readings of the north and south the same.

What would I find behind the door,
Would the room be splendid or bare and cold -
Would there be red carpet on the floor
Or perished silk in the curtain's fold?

What would I find if I bridged the moat,
And stood beside the castle wall -
Would a fanfare swell a triumphant throat
Or would the sharp portcullis fall?

What would I find if I climbed the stair
And faced you in your ivory tower -
Would there be roses for my hair
Or would you hold a withered flower?

Imperial lord, did I ignore your power
And walk my unsuspecting, quiet ways,
Forgetful of the fire and the flower,
Until you fused them in a bitter blaze
That burnt the pseudo-substitutes and left
A victory the victor could not gain,
A conquest that was total, but bereft
Of all the spoils of love, except the pain.
Imperial lord, if I forgot your force,
I shall not make the same default again,
Nor shall I try with trifles to divorce
The absolute completeness of your claim.
But it was harsh to purify with fire
A heart that dare not mention its desire.

How shall I love you, how shall I praise you,
Freshets of foam shall form lace for your hair,
Music shall startle the stars till they blaze you
Banners of beauty across the night air.
How shall I claim you, how shall I hold you,
Time has a passion for anything fair,
But sonnets have sinews with strength to enfold you,
Words have a power that Time cannot pare.
Present and missing, always and never,
Beauty and brilliance are breathing your breath,
This is a triumph beyond Time's endeavour,
This a force that is stronger than Death!
Inapprehensible pulsating glory,
Love ineluctable fashions your story.

FOR BARBY WHO IS IN LOVE WITH THE SUN - GOD

Sweet Night, take Barby in your healing arms
And shield her from the painful shafts of day,
Drop your deep peace upon the wild alarms
That shake her heart when light resumes full sway;
For she has dread of dawn and of the Sun
That mighty god, who with deliberate power
Forces her petals open one by one
And ravishes the darkness into flower.
She is the child of moonlight and of stars,
Of gentleness and clear pellucid skies,
And day's unwonted brilliance only mars
The subtleties embedded in her eyes.
Quick, claim her Night, before the passionate Sun
Attempts a beauty better left undone.

I went to the woods to find my love,
But I only found a tree,
And a jewel-bright bird that sang and said
"Thy love has gone from thee."

I slipped to the shore to find my love,
But I only found a stone,
And a silver shell that spoke and said,
"Thy heart is now alone."

I hied to the hills to find my love,
But I only found a mist,
And a mountain stream that splashed and said,
"Thy mouth is already kissed."

I ran to the rose to find my love,
But I only found a thorn,
And a glittering leaf that shook and said,
"Thy heart is forever torn."

Why did those words seem brighter than a jewel,
Fresher than flowers, fervent as a lark?
They led past caverns destined to be cruel,
Beneath a sun abetted by the dark.
Why did they seem as natural as wheat,
Richer than roses, delicate as frost?
They were the structure of their own defeat,
Of victory intending to be lost.
I heard you say them in a little room,
And even now the emptiness contains
The resurrection and the quick-sought tomb,
The dyad of your passion and your pains.
Oh, why should words so desperately fair,
Be but the pattern of their own despair?

Your feelings fall like stars across my heart,
To glance and glow and leave a lasting scar
Deep as the doubt that daunts you when we part,
The cicatrice but proves how wrong you are.
Your passion places leaves across my brow,
A laurel wreath with all the weight of yew,
And asphodels to teach the roses how
A fear can claim what only death is due.
To give and go, to love and leave, is void
Of that fulfillment faith alone supplies,
For hope increases, but to be destroyed,
And truth is tangled in a thousand lies.
Such stars and roses never were designed
For fear to force what love has failed to find.

Because we must not speak we never say
The words grown newly restless in our heart.
We keep those sweet sounds safely stored away,
And practise a precise and formal art.
We use no innuendoes, for our eyes
Have bared our single meaning and we know
The hesitant and heavenly surprise
Of mutual feeling that must never show.
And yet this silent harvest yields a grain
Sustaining as the very bread of life,
We gladly face the fasting, and the pain
Of separation thrusting like a knife:
It cannot cut the cords it cannot find,
That bind us thought to thought and mind to mind.

You were a shelter whose calm waters proved
A halcyon harbour for my reckless boat,
You were a giant tempests never moved
Although the storm had seized you by the throat.
You were a tree whose strong unyielding shade
Defeated winter with perennial spring,
You were an arbour whose compassion made
The bird superior to the broken wing.
You were a friend who never ceased to sift
The sands of feeling from the sea of love,
You were a guide who said the finest gift
Was that one never failed to give enough.
You were an alchemist who always knew
The dross was magic when the gold was true.

Had the double truth a double door
To shut out the shame and lock in the pride?
Had the double blackboard a double score
To prove to the heart that it hadn't lied?

Had the double meaning a double stair
That reached to heaven or dropped to hell?
Had the double devil a double snare
To make quite sure that the angel fell?

Annihilation
Hangs from a finger,
Before tomorrow
The hand may drop:
And only the dead
Will dare to linger
Beside a sorrow
No tear can stop.

For vacillation
Among the living,
Has failed to fetter
The threat above:
Held by the thread
Of utter giving,
It would be better
To die in love.

Canon Robert Winnett, Ph.D., D.D.

A churchman and a scholar and a friend
Is how so many think of you today.
A man whom disappointment could not bend
To anger or intolerant display.
A lover of the Classics and a man
Whose soul was stirred by great poetic art,
Who loved the sound of Latin, yet could plan
A sermon in short words that reached the heart.
An advocate of Johnson, one who knew
The moral writings of that mighty mind,
And found the Christian teaching flowered anew
Within the reverence his life defined.
An author of distinction, who would lend
His brilliant mind to counsel any friend.

Pain is conventional. We quickly learn
That sudden clouds may spoil a summer's day,
That fire is not the only flame to burn
Or steel the only substance that can slay.
Custom is with us and we soon discern
The actual from the abstract pang of pain,
The cruel extravaganza of concern,
The blood that won't resolve into a stain.
All this I knew, so did not stretch my hand
To pluck the briar roses where they grew,
Waiting for flowers I could understand
Whose purity seemed pledge that they were true:
But I have found the sharpest thorns in hell
Folded in lilies and wild asphodel.

SAMUEL JOHNSON

"The largest soul in England," Carlyle said,
The most extensive pattern of a man
Based on the cross where Christ's pale beauty bled
Into the mercy where all love began.
The most heroic and the most sincere,
Whose piety was constant, and whose mind
Worded the truths the whole world had to hear
In sentences a poet had designed.
Sam. Johnson, Ursa Major, The Great Cham!
Behind the names, the sovereign soul is there,
The lion strength that lay down with the lamb,
The virtues that were fortified with prayer.
The largest soul in England, and we claim
The overwhelming greatness of his name.

After the wine and wafer will there be
The feel of flesh and flowers that belong,
Or will a choir with candles offer me
The cloistered silence of receding song?
After the even pacing will I know
The sweet persuasion of an altered beat,
Or will Fate halt my haste and make me slow
The quick responses in my eager feet?
But why these feckless questions when I know
The answer is unvaried and the same,
My heartless task is but to watch love grow,
To catalogue its beauty and its pain,
To correlate refusal with request,
And confiscate the feeling in my breast.

Surely the rose should die when summer ends,
Its petals wither and its colour fade?
The safety of the coming buds depends
Upon the ritual of this cavalcade.
The glory of full summer learns to yield,
To bow before advancing winter's claim,
And valiantly retires from the field
Admitting there are limits to her reign.
But this despotic blossom rules my heart,
Entrenched, supreme, demanding and adored,
No future summer has a chance to start,
No coming winter could defeat this lord,
And I have found a season with the rose
Has absolutes no other summer knows.

SHAKESPEARE

"Not marble nor the gilded monuments
Of princes shall outlive this powerful rhyme."
Shakespeare sonnet 55

For Time's great rival with his massive brow,
His poetry, his passion and his prose,
Has kept the promise of his sonnet-vow,
And left us pages Time can never close.
For he has left us characters whose hope,
Whose ventures and whose vesture seem our own,
Who come to life again within the scope
Of genius that no other man has known.
And he has left us sonnets that proclaim,
In language that is vehement with power,
The knowledge that his writing would remain
Until our planet's last recorded hour.
What Time can not condemn, it must condone,
And Shakespeare has a mandate of his own.

FOR JACQUE

You lie not in the grave, but in my heart,
Your final resting place is not cold clay,
I tear the bonds of darkness far apart,
And clasp you closely to the light of day.
Through me, you feel again soft April's showers,
And see her cherry-trees break into lace,
And dream beneath her boughs of pleasant hours,
And feel her flowers fall upon your face.
Your lips flood into rose, your lids unveil
The sapphire beauty that no cloth can bind,
Your thoughts, your ways, yourself however pale,
Can find such recollection in my mind
You live again, oh Victory most sweet,
And Death himself acknowledges defeat!

SHAKESPEARE - POET SUI GENERIS

"Shall I compare thee to a summer's day?"
What summer's day could ever equal you?
The highest sun has not so bright a ray,
The darkest flower lacks so deep a hue.
And summer's song-birds, lark and nightingale,
That hymn the morning and enslave the night
Have found their fluted music can't prevail
Against the sound your sonnets set alight.
You are akin to nothing but your own
Sky-piercing height of manifold delight.
First poet of the world, immense, alone,
Cloud-crowned beyond our vision and our sight,
The songs you sing are of a breath so rare
The earth itself could not supply compare.

"Writing is an abuse of language."   Goethe.

Goethe was right! This sonnet should be heard
Close to your ear, so that my lips could stray
To meet your mouth, if there was any word
That only coupled contact could convey.
Goethe was right! This feeling should be sound,
Lilting and low, and murmurous as the blood
When it is quickened by the pulse's pound
And woos all waiting passion into flood.
Goethe was right! But when we are apart
Comparisons can only tantalize:
I cannot whisper words that rule my heart,
Or worship the concessions in your eyes.
So I am forced to write my song and hope
That symbols will abate what they evoke.

FOR EDWARD DARVALL

Edward Darvell's daughter, aged 19, was killed by a car.
He allowed her heart to be used in one of the first transplants in
South Africa. Unfortunately, the recipient also died.

This was your sacrifice, and her rare gift.
Unconquered by the carnage of it all
You fought for life, and with a thrust as swift
As sudden lightning, sought to lift the pall
From her young death by helping one to live.
The surgeons fought your battle and their own,
Till all had given all they had to give,
And love was planted and new hope had grown.
But now they both are dead, and you must feel
A double grief unique to you alone,
But sorrow at its zenith can't conceal
Your greater love upon its mighty throne.
Remember, when fresh memories compel,
You gave her heart. You gave your own, as well.

AUTUMN

Amber and apricot glow into view,
For nature is showing once more that she can
Alter the colour and capture the hue
Expected of autumn since seasons began.
Wood-smoke is pungent and apples are red,
Ground-frost has stencilled a chill in the air,
Summer admits that her flowers are dead,
Why does my heart still insist that I care?
When summer has ended, should autumn evoke
The pleasure and passion that summer laid bare,
The daisy-chain promise that suddenly broke,
The truth with its pattern of final despair?
But why chide the autumn? Each month of the year
Brings a remembrance I'm learning to fear.

SHAKESPEARE AND JOHNSON

Stratford and Lichfield, fortune-favoured towns,
Made famous by the birth of two great men
Whose thoughts and feelings broke all former bounds
And found the fruits of Paradise again.
Of two great men whose poetry and prose,
Whose lyric passion and whose moral stress
Adorns our England better than her rose,
And gilds her glory to a fine excess.
Shakespeare and Johnson, summits of our land
And viewed by other nations with acclaim,
Unrivalled leaders of that mighty band
Inscribed within the volume of our fame:
But gold and crimson letters cannot paint
Our greatest Poet and our greatest Saint.

SAMUEL JOHNSON

"Tell, for you can, by what unerring art
You wake to finer feelings every heart."

Arthur Murphy to Samuel Johnson.

A glowing tribute from a glowing friend,
Inspired by the virtue of your art.
A friend who from the first reading till the end
Extolled the noble vigour of your heart.
Who knew your Rambler essays and your Tracts,
Your Prologues, Poet's Lives and Sermons too,
And all the loyal, loving, tender acts
That brought the Christian tenets into view.
By writing and by precept and by deed
You opened hearts that then forgot to close,
Because they felt the pressure of a creed
Whose beauty was as thrilling as a rose,
And found, through the magnificence of art,
The unexampled splendour of your heart.

SAMUEL JOHNSON

"There is something in Samuel Johnson
That needs no protection."
Ralph Waldo Emerson.

Ralph Waldo Emerson could write great praise
In inverse ratio to the words he used,
Until the silent sounds found force to raise
A fire and flame that suddenly was fused
Into a burning truth, and we would find
The close-cut words had power to graze our heart
And carve a deep impression in our mind,
For Emerson was saying, with fine art,
The highest of high praise could never reach
The plateau where great Johnson paced apart.
His virtue made a wall no foe could breach
For honour was instinctive from the start.
His genius was invincible and he
Was greater than our utmost praise could be.

FOR NAVY - LIEUTENANT NICHOLAS TAYLOR

"I am proud to have a son who died doing the job he loved, for the country he loved."

Harry Taylor.

Your noble words have echoed in our heart.
We share your sorrow and we share your pride.
And though at first you felt the harsh tears start,
In time a kinder feeling will preside
And loss will find a leveller in love
With all its vivid memories of your boy,
That youngster who had set his eyes above
To gain the skies and know a flyer's joy.
But sterner duties called him and he left
Knowing the perils that now lay ahead.
He gave his life and left your own bereft,
And yet his shining courage is not dead,
For you have found the words to give it life
Above the carnage of this bitter strife.

Gladys Sandes FRCS England
1897 - 1968

A woman of high purpose, and firm resolve,
of conquering intellect and profound humanity.

Not until now, although I thought I knew
Every advantage of your love and care,
Could I assess my ceaseless debt to you,
Who conquered a crescendo of despair.
Not until now, when Death has sealed your eyes,
Have I found sight to penetrate the will,
Inflexible, beneath the dear disguise
Of kindliness that cloaked consummate skill.
Not until now, and with so full a force,
Imperative and absolute and true,
Could I appraise the bounty of a course
That shaped my life so I should come to you.
But poetry is powerless to pay
The gamut of my gratitude today.

S L U M S

How can the heart expand enclosed in these
Embarassed crumblings of another age,
Bare bricks without the modesty of trees,
But with the latent power of a cage?

How can the mind grow straight against the slant
Of Pisa-like indifference and dirt?
Where is the earth to root the reaching plant,
Or space to take the tendrils without hurt?

How can the child of shadow learn to stand
Undaunted, not defiant, in the sun?
So small a sacrifice would take his hand
And coax his lips to rivulets of fun.

No chestnut tree was lovelier in the world
When you stood pierced with blossoms, unafraid,
No passion of green glory yet unfurled
Could equal the magnificence you made.
No offering of more beauty to the mind
Was ever spread before the human eye,
No greater grace in winter could one find
Than your bare branches flung against the sky.
And you were proof against all hands but time
Until some mindless mortal cut you down -
Such lack of comprehension was a crime
That placed another thorn in Christ's crown -
Yet held within my love you still stand strong,
And all your branches tremble with birds' song.

Does time set certain buds for certain springs,
And match each summer with its fated flower?
Do swallows wait the undisputed wings
Elected by their unrenouncing hour?
Are winds wrapped in a dream until they blow
One destined petal from one special rose?
Are oaks content in acorns till they grow
The predetermined leaf their season knows?
If this is so, why am I faced with you?
What wayward date has brought the noonday sun
To scorch my twilight, and to make less true
The aberrant moment when we were begun?
If only love could telescope the years,
And adoration lose the need for tears.

I shall recall the delight
Securely based on rock,
But not the sands of longing
Or the tide's cruel shock.

I shall remember the laughter
And the unprotected line
Of your upper lip's quiescence
In our most gentle time.

And I shall find my anguish
Drowned in a flood long past,
Leaving gulls of gladness
On oceans that will last.

For Dr. Frank Spracklen

Truth found and extension in your face,
And gentleness had brushed you with strong wings
That left the feather-pattern of a grace
As lovely as the green that April brings.
Compassion was related to your eyes
And laughter loved the corner of your lips,
The strong sun of your courage was a prize
You gladly shared with those in pain's eclipse.
And I was in a night divorced from dawn,
A tearing darkness that in some way seemed
A deathly game of love, with me as pawn
Both to despair and to the hope I dreamed.
And you were grave and kind, because you knew
The flowers of the spirit are so few.

HARRY HUNKS

This day I saw Harry Hunks, a blind and weeping bear,
whipped by six men until the blood ran down his shoulders.

Visitor to London, 16th Century.

Four centuries have passed between your pain
And my dismay, and yet my mind can hear
The cruel vociferation of your name
Within the dark arena of your fear.
Four centuries, and still the stinging whips
Sing in my head, and the neglected tears
From the blind eyes are salt upon my lips,
As Pity, reinstated, reappears.
Pity, too late to succour or to save,
Belated, but beloved, change of heart,
Pity that cannot reach you in the grave
And so expends its tenderness in Art.
Pity that hears and feels your vanished pain,
And kneels before your courage and our shame!

The winter held my love in check
As plants are bound by ice,
But spring has made a flimsy wreck
Of such a brash device,
For she has flung a flower here
And tossed a song-bird there
And blown a message quick and clear
Into the melting air,
And I have felt the clots of pain
Impact my new-found heart -
The rites of spring invite in vain
If you will not take part.

I didn't know
That love could be
Such concentrated
Agony,
Or that its searching
Deadly flame
Preserved the petal
In the pain.

I didn't know
That longing grew
Until it tore
The heart in two,
Or that it fired
The helpless brain
With images
It couldn't claim.

I didn't know
That lust could be
Devil denied
Divinity,
Or that the wine
Of passion's waste
Was quite so monstrous
To the taste.

The Flower Portrait of Shakespeare has been shown, on X-ray, to have
been painted over an Italian canvas of The Virgin and Child.

"There's a divinity that shapes our ends,"
So wrote the Star of Poets, for he knew
The cosmic current when the dove descends
Has power to overwhelm or reconstrue.
There's providence in every sparrow's fall,
Although the opposite might well seem true,
When little feathered throats no longer call
Their bird-hosannas to the heaven's blue.
Love's ultimate can not be seen in part,
Though in the finished pattern will prevail
The final judgement of the final heart,
And so the destined artist did not fail,
But chose to paint a worth no world could price,
On gentle Mary and the waiting Christ.

SHAKESPEARE

You caught the wind and pushed the clouds aside,
Harnessed the moon and showed the glowing sun
The white-rose radiance of the star-crossed bride
Effulgent as the day and night in one.
You shook a million petals from the May,
And lured the loveliness from every flower,
You found they were the words you had to say
To prove your love's felicity and power.
You counselled kings, and then replaced the sage,
You wrote swift songs for merry, passing bands,
You honoured honour, and on every page
Your adamant nobility still stands,
That ages yet unborn may live to find
The unassaulted beauty of your mind.

FOR DR. SERGE BAROLD

If she could see you now she would feel proud
As any mother might of such a son.
(Her vision isn't sheltered by a shroud
It shattered at the point of Nazi gun).
If she could see you now she still would trace
The vivid child proclaiming such a man.
(But Nazi culture strangely lacked the grace
Displayed to women since the world began).
Her death was anguish, for how could she tell
There burnt within the breast of one pale nun
A flame of love to rout the powers of hell,
And dare the sweet salvation of her son?
Now, working as a doctor, you repay
The undivided mercy of that day.

SONNET FOR A ROSE

Passionate beauty that we call a rose,
How can a poet find words to convey
Deep crimson petals that curve and unclose
Fragrance an angel has hidden away?
Absolute ecstasy poised in the air,
Lilacs and lilies are blossoming too,
But yours is a loveliness past all compare,
Each other flower owes homage to you.
Darker than dahlias, or burning like phlox,
Sweeter than myrtles, more famous than bay,
Solacing sorrow wherever death knocks,
Ardent with honour, what more can I say?
That which has placed you all others above,
Emblem of England and symbol of love.

PROFESSOR WILLIAM J. MAYHEAD

You would have been his choice if he had lived
Within the noisy clamour of our days
And sought to find a person who could give
Full volume to the music of his plays.
You would have been the one that he would choose
To adumbrate his gold and silver thought,
To show the crown nobility can't lose
Or prove the gems of honour can't be bought.
For Shakespeare blended three quite separate spheres
To make the dazzling circle of his art,
And this three-fold effulgence reappears
Within the shining knowledge you impart.
In Shakespeare, heart and soul and mind agree,
And you reflect this lovely trinity.

"The hope of happiness is so strongly impressed,
that the longest experience is not able to efface it."

Samuel Johnson.

We know it may not happen, yet we hope
However often hope has turned to tears,
For happiness would give our heart full scope,
Release our talents and refute our fears.
We hope another year will set things right,
And cancel the betrayals of the past,
That now we can unloose our soul in flight
Secure within a passion that will last.
We never learn! The hope is always there
And sanctions false belief in what will be,
That clouds will clear and when the day is fair
We shall enjoy a new felicity.
And even when life proves that we are wrong,
We still believe the singer and the song.

Not even Love with all his flowers,
And foaming branches of white May,
Can quite repeal the fatal hours
That stole my coming wedding-day.
Not even Love with his rich mouth,
And lips of honey-nectar sweet,
Can thaw the frost with all his south,
And make my summer quite complete.
A crippled Bride I must remain,
But one who in her sorrow knows,
The tenderness that comes from pain,
The dark indulgence of the rose,
And all the honours of the bed
Where Love lay proudly garlanded.

Jewels could not contain this loss,
Their recompense is simply measured.
This was a waste no wave can toss
On to sands more deeply treasured.

I speak of the ruined time you thought
Would act as compost for a rose
Incomparable, without a spot,
Whose open heart would never close.

But time can not be stored to make
Two summers' roses into one,
And I am left with roots that ache
For what was only half-begun.

HOMAGE TO A SPANIARD

It was your grace that made it perilous -
I could have parried tenderness and wit,
But this was subtle-sweet and singular
My startled heart had no defence for it.

For this was grace pervasive as a thought,
Intangible, and yet immensely real,
More delicate than ashes, though it held
The fatal strength of old Toledo steel.

Sweet Lord, send me defeat of all things dear,
Dear eyes, dear hands, dear movements and dear mouth,
Conquer them for me, though it leaves me drear
As barren north denied the beauteous south.
Prove this the final anguish of my heart
For love is now contiguous to pain,
And I am crucified when memories start
And know the crucifixion is in vain.
Grant me emancipation from the dream
That ravishes my life with fatal ease,
The rosy dream that's stronger than a beam
Of mighty oak from one of England's trees.
A conquest, Lord, of this destructive heaven,
The bread of life without this grievous leaven.

SHAKESPEARE'S GRAVE - HOLY TRINITY CHURCH

The stained-glass window sheds a purple light
That glows like violets on his sombre tomb.
Once, living violets gave a sharp delight
To that rich mind no darkness can consume.
But even as I watch the colour grows
And deepens to the royal hue of kings
In tribute to a majesty that rose
Above regalia to immortal things.
And still the colour alters and I see
The primal purple of the prism's plane,
Part of a rainbow sequence that could be
Symbolic of his passion and his pain,
For every colour in the world combined
Upon the palette of this poet's mind.

SHAKESPEARE

"From the four corners of the earth they come,
To kiss this shrine.....

                    Merchant of Venice.

From the four corners of the earth they come
To kiss this shrine with overflowing heart,
Their feelings speaking though their lips are dumb
Before such vast pre-eminence of art.
From every corner and from every land
The willing, eager, gladsome throng arrive,
Drawn by the power of that immortal hand
Whose words are still compellingly alive.
They proffer thanks for poetry and plays,
For thoughts of such swift beauty that their flight
Can make an incandescence in their days
Or improvise a starlight in their night.
They come to pay him homage, but far more
They come to love, to honour and adore.

VILLANELLE

Because I love you I could let you go,
Although I dreaded what the days would bring,
Knowing the swiftest hour would be slow.

And though my heart reverberates with woe,
Remembering kisses sweeter than the spring,
Because I love you I could let you go,

And face the fact that time would never grow
Into a moment when our hands could cling,
Knowing the swiftest hour would be slow.

Yet conscious of an even fiercer foe,
The interdict on letters from my King,
Because I love you I could let you go.

And recognize no future would bestow
A love that made each lazy moment sing,
Knowing the swiftest hour would be slow,

But knowing, too, that time will surely show
My sonnets hold you in their magic ring.
Because I love you I could let you go,
Knowing the swiftest hour would be slow.

The petals falling from the falling rose,
Hold, for that moment, all their summer's prime,
Even in dissolution, they disclose
The harmony consistent with that time.
The sound still ringing when the bell has rung,
Still celebrates a moment past compare,
The sound still singing when the song is sung,
Vibrates with all the beauty of the air.
And neither change nor chance can take away
That rare extravaganza in the past,
That sweet indulgence has the power to stay
Within a factual-fusion that will last,
And in the fixed eternity of time,
Your love remains inseparable from mine.

A COMPLAINT TO WILLIAM SHAKESPEARE

You wrote because you had to, and to please
My Lord Southampton and the Virgin Queen.
You wrote to give tormented passion ease,
And prove the peacock's feathers feared by Greene!
You wrote to honour England, and to show
The universal intricate of pain.
You wrote to capture laughter and the woe
Of feelings at their greatest when in vain.
You wrote to be remembered, and your lines
Come thrilling through the throats of many lands.
You stay the soul, the wonder of all times,
But what, within the complex of such plans,
Made you project your manhood with your art,
And claim the future roses of my heart?

FOR MY SON,

ON FIRST SEEING A PICTURE OF HIS SON.

Beside this picture, palaces dissolve,
This is a wealth that cancels that of Kings,
Within this head, a universe evolves,
Within this heart, a resurrection rings.
Beside this treasure, gold is set at nought,
Against this fortune, diamonds weigh in vain,
This is the innocence that man forgot
Become the wine that love can never drain.
This, above all, is life's supremest gift,
This is an answering as sweet as Spring,
This is an anchor that can never drift
Into a sea of doubt and wondering.
This is your son, both powerful and weak,
This is the utmost any search can seek.

"Good frend for Iesus sake forbeare
To digg the dust encloased heare:
Bleste be ye man yt spares thes stones
And curst be he yt moves my bones."

Shakespeare.

I shall not move the bones or peerless dust,
Commanded by my love and not your curse,
Obedient to a reverence that must
Annul the need for death-inscripted verse.
Safe-sacrosanct your grave remains from me,
But I, in turn, am threatened by your mind
That moves my heart to such a high degree
There's hazard in the beauty that I find.
With words you formed an eagle of delight
That soared beyond our world's periphery
And, falling from an unrepeated height,
Released the feathers of divinity.
Inviolate still stays your noble rest,
The tremor is the tumult in my breast.

Another summer brings another scene
Identical to those of summers past,
With all the roses of what might have been,
And daisy-chains too delicate to last.
Another summer brings another sigh
As fragrant as the clover in the grass,
And eyes that speak, but offer no reply,
Like echoes caught within a chill crevasse.
Another summer that will never end
In autumn glory or fast falling fruit,
An isolated season of pretend
With feelings flying, but denied pursuit.
A trellissed-rose that climbs, but must not clamber,
And thoughts of love confined, like pearls in amber.

Was the ocean too wide for love to span,
Was the parting too long for love to hold,
Was fidelity woman and fickleness man,
Was the lamb betrayed in the shepherd's fold?

Was the love too strong to accept a ghost,
Was the love too strong to let it go,
Was the least adored 'till it grew the most,
Was the heart destroyed by its own bright flow?

Was the dream too vivid for him, for her,
Was the moment grazed by eternity,
Was desire sharpened by absence's blur,
Was loved saved and drowned by the tossing sea?

A spider could not spin so fine a thread
As that which binds our hearts each time we meet,
And angels never went with softer tread
Than we towards a love so incomplete.
A nightingale could scarcely find the note
That we persuade ourselves we do not hear,
Though tenderness is welling in our throat
And silence never sang a song so clear.
And yet this unkept promise is a jewel
More precious than the rubies in a crown,
An iridescent moment that can fool
Realities that weigh our purpose down,
For we have found with sensitive surprise
The gift of gladness in each other's eyes.

The sharp, sweet smell of autumn cleaves the air
And careless trees drop gold beneath my feet.
The bush that held the rose is in despair,
And berries cluster in a bright conceit.
The glowing grass is streaked with faded dun
And rough brown bark has crevices of pink
That still respond in beauty to the sun,
Although he moves towards the winter's brink.
All this my senses show me and my mind
Is grateful for the loveliness I see,
But nowhere in the landscape can I find
A transposition of identity.
My mind rejoices and my senses thrill,
But lacking you, my heart is strangely still.

I cannot reconstruct from aught I know
The God-like benediction of your hand,
In that rich clasp I felt my whole world blow
To atoms in an ecstasy of sand.
Yet what divine destruction, for it made
Me lose myself to find myself in you,
A paradise that time can never fade
Nor any other heaven make less true.
Inexorably, perdition took its toll,
Exacted to a tittle what was due,
Left me my heart without its pulse's roll,
A ghost who only comes to life for you.
Your love would force my fate's extremest bars
And lift me to an ecstasy of stars.

Dull passive clouds of soft unceasing grey,
Cancel the azure drifting in my sky.
Cover my conquest, caution me to stay
Within the mists that solace such as I.
Defensive clouds so distant yet so near,
Send me a storm to kill this kindling fire,
Or else a wind that's strong enough to veer
And block the straight direction of desire.
For this time, unlike others, I am prone
To claim the vivid centre of the rose,
To purloin what has now become my own,
And pay the price disclosure will disclose.
Oh, hide this fatal flower that makes me bold,
For if I grasp, no fear shall loose my hold.

A 27TH SONNET FOR THE DARK LADY

EMILIA BASSANO, was it you?
Were yours the eyes that Shakespeare so mis-read?
Were yours the scarlet ornaments that drew
The Swan of Avon from his marriage-bed?
Were yours the sonnet-celebrated hands
That sway'd the wiry concord of the keys?
I find no tender inward to the bands
That brought the Star of Poets to his knees.
Oh pity-wanting woman, you can claim
The taut and tortured roses of his lust,
The story of your sonnets is the shame
Of passion turned to frenzy, lacking trust:
And centuries have waited for the name
They did not want to honour, but to blame!

I would get through the thickest hedge of thorn
A thousand spears should block my path in vain,
And I would glory in my flesh cruel torn
And wear the laurels of my spear-thrust pain.
The darkest wood could scarcely daunt my entry,
I would not halt for river in full spate,
The castle of my faith would need no sentry,
My love would be quite shadowless of hate;
And yet I can't get through the mists of fear
That fall like tears around your beating heart,
The phoenix of my fire can't seem to clear
The barrier that keeps our lives apart.
Oh let love lead you to the waiting throne,
So I can bring the roses you have grown.

SONNET FOR THE SILENT

Have I found words for what you longed to say
And caught the thoughts your tongue could never trap?
Are you refreshed by my far fountain's spray,
And does my rose drop petals in your lap?
Have I released a rush of mountain air
To cool the heated hollow of your brow?
Have I found phrases that you find as fair
As what you feel, but never could avow?
It is the Poets's devoir and delight
To speak for those who feel, but cannot say,
To kindle words until they can ignite
The barriers that hold the heart at bay,
To offer fresh-found freedoms and relieve
The many inarticulates who grieve.

HOSANNA FOR ENGLAND

What can I say that Shakespeare has not said
For ever and for always in the speech
He granted dying Gaunt? What thought unsped
By that quick quill can I attempt to reach
In praise of England? What facet of the stone
Securely set in Shakespeare's silver sea
Could I re-cut in words that were my own
And not be guilty of immodesty,
Unless I praise a praise he did not know,
That gathers power every passing year,
A glory and a gladness that still grow,
A triumph without parallel or peer,
That out of all the nations of the earth,
This demi-paradise gave Shakespeare birth.

The peony of love is closed,
Its petals folded fast within,
The pull of summer quite opposed
Its lovely colour drained and dim.
There was a June that once laid bare
The utmost passion of its heart,
Celestial June without compare
That made all other Junes depart,
And left a frost so hard and white
No other blooming could begin,
No other opening to delight
Or petals touching heaven's rim,
But fatal flower shut in night
Although the sun shines fierce and bright.

SHAKESPEARE

To walk beside the Avon and to feel
The glory that is gliding with the swan,
The immanence no darkness can conceal,
The miracle recurrent with the dawn:
To wander by the willows and to know
In former times he watched such branches bend
And felt their sad and lonely greeness so,
They served as temple for Ophelia's end:
To be in his sweet Stratford, and to send
To sky and grass and trees and earth and stone,
Acknowledgement of beauty without end
In passion simultaneous with his own,
Can tear the very centuries apart
And sacrifice my senses to his heart.

It may be in another world,
That I shall pay for this,
Balance in pain and sorrow
This overplus of bliss.
Exchange for withered flowers
The blossom of his mouth,
Barter my soul's live water
For thirst unslaked and drouth.
Give up his flesh's sweet warmness
For garments harsh and cold,
Return his silver laughter
For tears unplumbed, untold.
What ransom could be heavy,
What price too full of sighs,
To equal the ecstasy I knew
When stars fell from his eyes?

Words could make us clumsy, they could be
False paths that lead us further from the rose
That's opening in the vivid privacy
The deep-walled garden of our passion knows.
Words could make us brittle, they could break
The spun-glass bridge that reaches our desire,
And leave us no alternative to take
Us nearer to the all-beseeching fire.
Now is the time to let the pulses reign,
They beat a message love can understand,
They place the throbbing centre of my pain
Within the sweet enclosure of your hand.
The body is a clear and constant star
To show our heart exactly where we are.

Why must I with divided eyes
See both what is and what could be,
When Love so lightly could devise
A single-visioned ecstasy?

Why must I with a parted breast
Pretend I do not feel the thorn,
A thousand roses unpossessed
Had never left my heart so torn!

Mine was a grief you did not want to see
For it out-suffered sonnets and became
The living, not the lyric, agony,
The furnace truth behind the altar flame.
Mine was a pain you did not mean to free
For it disrupted mountains and you found
The summits of your true divinity
Sharp as the passion of my broken ground.
Oh! hell is truth confounded by itself
Beyond the heaven of a monstrous lie,
The roughest poison hidden on life's shelf
Were tender if it promised I should die.
No greater sacrifice have I to give
Than, wanting death, I still elect to live.

This faith moved mountains, for it drained the seas
To make sweet lakes on lonely high plateaus,
Transplanted forests and arranged the breeze
To open every petal of the rose;
Discovered valleys that had never been
Without the gentle closure of their leaves,
And brought bright flowers from another scene
In case the present pastures failed to please.
This faith moved mountains with so slight a touch
That everything seemed part of a design,
The lovely less, the perfect over-much,
That love and loss and life and death combine.
This faith moved mountains, but it could not part
The gossamer reluctance of your heart.

The flowers are <u>for</u> us. Everywhere I look
Five simple petals form to make a star,
And from Christ's clock the very wisest took
Establishment of miracles that are.
The trees are for us. Even the sternest bough
Is reconciled to sweet unfolding green,
And surely such fixed sufferance must allow
The hope of hearts surrendered and serene?
And yet, despite these signs, we seem to be
Forever poised to fly from what we feel,
And, balanced like the two tides of the sea,
Alternately we cover and reveal.
Is there no wave to hurl us to a shore
Where love can build its altar and adore?

My body's in a state of civil war,
My heart and mind at constant enmity
Within a realm that was their peace before
Love placed them in such sore extremity.
Protagonists of equal strength they stand
Strong-armoured with a different point of view,
And one's cold reasoning can not expand
To hold the burning hope the other knew.
My mind, with all the power of painful thought,
Has loosed such logic arrows that despair
Has pierced my heart, already overwrought
By contact with a grace beyong compare:
And I, the twofold victim of their strife,
Adore the cause that keeps contention rife.

Some winters only curl the buds they freeze
Into a stronger pattern for the spring,
But others, with intense severities,
Destroy resurgence with resuffering.
And then, although the tree may later wear
The reassurance of unnumbered leaves,
The nerves stay numb, beyond the sun's repair,
Sealed in a frost of icy cruelties.
But there are other gods besides the sun,
And grace has power to thaw as well as heat,
And gentleness can bind what was undone,
And homage melt the rigours of defeat:
And ice, still solid though the wind blew south,
Dissolved against the summer of your mouth.

ON SEEING THE ORIGINAL DOOR IN SHAKESPEARE'S BIRTHPLACE

This door met Shakespeare's hand. His fingers knew
The impress of its graining and its strength.
I touched it now and felt as though it drew
My love along time's intervening length.
This door took Shakespeare's weight. He must have leant
Against its fond support in former days.
The burden of my love is now content
To rest upon four hundred years of praise.
This door was Shakespeare's, but that other door
He opened so humanity could see
Each truth made brighter and all love made more,
Was one for which he, only, held the key.
But through the consummation of his art
It proved the key to every human heart.

Oh, let me press these petals to my face!
Make this my summer, for so many springs
Have failed to find a passion and a grace
Effulgent as the rose this season brings.
Oh, let it make a garden in my breast!
Though foreign to the soil from which it grew,
Its dark, demanding beauty brings me rest
And ecstasies my spirit never knew.
This is a love trans-patterned from the past
Into the pulsing present, and its songs
Have made the nightingale iconoclast
In the carved temple where the voice belongs.
Oh, let me shrine this rose for my life's span,
I've waited for it since the world began.

Must there be blood at birth and grinding pain,
The soul enveloped in unyielding flame,
When lilies are responsive to the rain
Could we not train our roses to the same?
Must distance lend velocity to love
And discipline impeach the flowering mouth,
Beside wells of sweet silver, must we prove
The aching, ardent agony of drouth?
Oh love needs no such guard and no such test,
It is the balance of its own rich load,
It holds or gives as ecstasy knows best
Without the imperfection of a goad.
Love is untidy when its growth is free,
And absolute with perfect symmetry.

You skim across the contours of my mind,
A transient figure of such innate grace,
I half-forgive a torture that's designed
To keep me hungry-thirsty for your face:
To make me want those love-defying eyes
That closed me in a circle of desire,
Those lips, whose curve extended Paradise
And added a new string to Orpheus' lyre.
Why must you force the caverns of the past
And light the ardent candles of false hope,
Pretending, in a blaze that cannot last,
To reconcile the passion you revoke?
Oh harsh exacerbation of despair
That disappointment claims a source so fair.

I thought I knew the stream of love
The shallow and the deep,
I thought I knew its binding banks
The even and the steep,
I thought I knew the way it ran
Straight-flowing or a-swirl,
I thought its clearest waters held
The coral and the pearl.

I thought I knew the way of love
Its follies and its feints,
I thought I knew its rosary
Its devils and its saints,
I thought I knew its images
Its splendour and its prayer,
But I have found it can be bound
To gods no longer there.

This was the chrysalis of my delight,
Within these walls a fatal fever flamed
That lit our feelings to a dazzling height
And adumbrated what love hadn't claimed.
We were the flotsam of time's stringency,
Our pattern quickened to the measured flow
Of minutes streaming past relentlessly
Towards the hour when you would have to go.
And now the room is like a skeleton
Without the flesh of love or blood of wit,
A lifeless structure that I hasten from
Amazed to find that memory doesn't fit.
These bricks were incidental to the fact
Of your mind reaching mine in burning pact.

I can't accept this artificial death,
I feel my heart beat on, my eyes still see,
My lungs release their grief in natural breath,
My lips retain our passion's mystery.
My brain is sentient and the restless cells
Review the manuscript of memory
With such exactitude that truth impels
Resistance to this false catastrophe.
Love is alive, although you call it dead
And relegate it to an unseen tomb,
And place the golden circle of your head
Within the cruel circumference of doom.
Is love so full of terror that you crave
The dismal reassurance of the grave?

That almond spray, which with slow pride doth start,
Its blossom tribute to the coming Spring,
Can find no matching answer in my heart,
But buds tight-closed, without their sun to bring
His sweet unsealing warmth that would unfold,
The final petal from the final hold.

That bird which sings as though he had no care,
But to make perfect carol for the sun,
Has never known the wild and dark despair,
Of flowers that wither for the lack of one,
Oh Love, my Sun, you could with one swift dart,
Begin the private Spring within my heart.

I'm glad you found me worthy of the truth,
It added laurel to a crown of thorn,
It twined the bitterness with strands of ruth
And stitched the ragged hole your words had torn:
For truth alone possessed the power to part
The figures turning in the bubble-dream,
To synchronize the scalpel with the heart
And separate the symbol from the scheme.
Astringent truth that staunched the stinging flow
Of memory's deep currents through my mind,
Curetting truth that scraped the surface so
The heart was healthy and the flesh could bind.
The truth was piercing, for your blade was keen,
The wound was torment, but the wound was clean.

Oh, give me any answer but the hum
Of throbbing silence - I should prefer an oath,
For that would prove your feelings were not numb,
Although it proved the self-same source was loath.
Or stab me with the accents of contempt
That shape your lips with such divine disdain,
I worship what you most would keep exempt,
The lovely scimitars that cause my pain.
But is the choice of anger or of scorn,
Are there not sweeter measures you could take,
Have they not won the rose who wear the thorn
Deep in a side made humble for your sake?
Only repeat the words that once you said,
Carelessly breathing life into the dead.

Where did you find the yardstick that you use
To calculate exactitude in love?
And where the false barometer you choose
To keep the pressure equal to the dove?
And what new valve have you installed to stop
The rising volume of the pulse's pound?
And by what subtle magic can you drop
From breathless heights to safety on the ground?
Oh, there is something monstrous in the art
That measures feeling like a pound of rice,
For such severe reluctance of the heart
Is worse than a whole calendar of vice,
For no crime is so grave as that which seeks
To pay the valley's ransom with the peaks.

We who were prodigal with song
Shall now be mute our whole life long,
Self-immolation of the strong.

We who preferred perfection to
The rosemary that mixed with rue
Have closed our calyx to the dew.

We who felt all our passions move
Into a life-appointed groove
Have nothing left that we need prove.

The earth was meant to hold the seed
Not to make feet of clay;
Women find the gods they need
In quite another way.

They do not look for burnished shield
Or laurels on the brow;
They watch the lilies of the field
Perpetuate their vow.

The earth was meant to hold the seed
Safe and dark and deep;
That is the way the gods are freed
That is the tryst they keep.

Was the feeling deep,
Or did it lie
Within the orbit
Of your eye:
Those clever eyes
That you had taught
To hold the answer
That I sought?

Was the song for two,
Or did your throat
Refuse to take
The final note:
Because you felt
That harmony
Was safer in
A minor key?

Which of us cheated,
You or I
Or did the true
Imbalance lie
In making light
Of what was real
And saying words
We did not feel?

FOR HEMINGE AND CONDELL

They were his fellows, and within his Will
He stipulated sums to buy them rings
That tokens of his fellowship might fill
Part of the gap that total absence brings.
They were his fellows, and he loved them well,
They understood his mind, and he their ways,
And when they heard the surly sullen bell
And knew that he had numbered all his days,
They clasped their hands and vowed that he should live,
Despite the rigid confines of the grave:
They published plays humanity would give
The recompense of centuries of praise.
And yet so overwhelming is our debt
There is some danger that it can't be met.

"I WAS A FORGET-ME-NOT
IN SHAKESPEARE'S GARDEN".

He chose his roses and his lilies, too,
His peonies, his pansies and his phlox,
His daffodils with bugles filled with dew,
His tenderly pervasive gillistocks.
He ordered violets and passion-flowers
And marigolds with great dark sleepy eyes,
And lavender with all her purple powers,
And rosemary entangled with his sighs.
He asked for columbine as well as clover,
And crocuses, those heralds of the spring,
But when his choice of love was nearly over,
He saw the youngest child look questioning,
And finding her the dearest of the lot,
He took her for his own forget-me-not.

Melissa left her blossoms for your lips,
Refused the Rose and passed the fragrant May,
Denied the Honeysuckle her sweet sips
And told the Lily she could not delay.
Ignored the Pansy with her pleading face
And disengaged the clinging Eglantine,
For nowhere in her flowers could she trace
A honey-dew intoxicant as wine.
If you seduce a Goddess, how can I,
A mortal with a woman's fraility,
Release my mounting longing with the sigh
That I do not deserve such ecstasy?
Small wonder if my resolution slips,
Melissa left her blossoms for your lips.

Rain has a privacy that lets me dream
Extravagant and unsubstantial things,
Reality's stark glare is but a gleam
Beside my fancy's iridescent wings.

In slanting mist, stern distance soon dissolves,
Your fingers reach towards my willing hand,
I feel you close, and your warm breath resolves
The fear that clips me like an iron band.

And nothing is, but what I want to be,
And love becomes as natural as the rain,
Your eyes reflect my passion's gravity,
Your gentleness extinguishes my pain.

When you have gone away and other eyes
Drown in that blue which still is heaven to me,
When you are no more here and other hands
Entwine those fingers that were mine to free,
When all my days are barren of your smile,
And even dreams are empty of your kiss,
I should to memory's store adjourn a while
In retrospect to steal the joys I miss,
But love, dare I remember that my body once knew spring
In that cruel winter when no birds shall sing?

AUTUMN

This season, more than others, pricks my heart
And lances sentience with so sharp a knife,
That blood becomes confederate with art,
And death becomes analogous to life.
For in this time of falling leaf and smoke,
Of pungent petals punishing the air,
The faintest twinge of perfume can evoke
An anguish too elaborate to bear.
And then the simple branches stretched like spars,
The stubble with its embassies of hay,
The orange berries fastened with black stars
Are intricates of beauty and dismay.
And quickened by quiescence my heart grieves,
Despite the lovely anodyne of leaves.

This love-voltaic energy that must
Be turned from its objective to become
A patina of beauty in the dust,
A laurel leaf alive when lips are dumb.
This ardent stream of feeling that should flow
Into the eager cavern of your heart,
Must be deflected so you cannot know
Its power and its passion, save in art.
This transmutation of a gold to gold,
This fair exchange of apples on a tree,
Is triumph with its misery untold,
Is conquest with its bitter victory.
Oh, futile alchemy that could suppose
To reinstate the heaven of a rose.

Dark eyes and hair stern-banished from my heart,
Why do you come this April with the sun?
Evocative of memories that now start
Opening like flowers, slowly one by one.
I think you would not haunt me if you knew,
There was so much I made myself forget,
So much too beautiful the memory grew
Even to be remembered, and oh yet,
Dear God, I still remember that proud head
So painfully forgotten, and oh drouth,
Oh thirst whose power will parch me till I'm dead,
The perfect imperfection of that mouth.

So sweet a gift to be so seldom given,
But by infrequency not made more dear
Than its intrinsic worth, which now lies hidden
Beneath the heavy wrappings of your fear:
Encloaking fear that folds you in a mist
Of nebulous uncertainty that racks,
Miasmal murder, which you don't resist
Because reality has fiercer facts,
And yet that same reality could hold
A sun to melt an avalanche of pain,
A sun whose golden fingers would unfold
The fibres closed so tight against the rain;
Oh leave this lethal fog, for you have won
The limitless potential of the sun.

TO A WEST INDIAN CHILD IN HOSPITAL

Small, mute and dark, you sit within your chair,
A failing patient from a foreign land,
Threading a scarlet ribbon in your hair
With nervous movements of your brown bird hand.

Yours is a fatal case - you'll not grow tall
To move with ancient grace about your world,
The green leaf of your childhood will be all
The fleeting plant of life can force unfurled.

You scarcely know I saw you, as you sit
Beyond the healing circle of our art,
Stretched to the touch of death's cruel fingertip,
But held within the circle of my heart.

There is an equilibrium in love
That finds the spirit level of the whole,
That balances the eagle with the dove
And counter-weights the leaves against the bole.
There is a generosity of heart
That multiplies by self-dividing cell,
A myriad amoeba that can start
A tide too mighty for the moon to quell;
For there can be preponderance in love,
A forest growing for one flower's shade,
Adoring lips are ravished by the glove
That masks the tender palm their kisses crave.
An ocean can respond to one small tear,
It is indifference that shapes love's bier.

This rose you give, this lovely phantom flower,
Deep-petalled, fragrant, passionate as dawn,
Has learned to live beyond our floral hour
And find fresh buds for me to dote upon.
This rose you give, this lovely idle flower,
Careless as rain, persuasive as the sun,
Employs new means to emphasize its power
And burns an incense that is never done.
This rose you leave is not a fleeting flower,
Forgotten forfeit of a moment's grace,
No worm within the garden can devour
The memory of attar on my face.
This rose we share will still prevail, though you
Release the roots that it is fastened to.

Joy has cried wolf too often. Now I feel
A disbelief so sweeping, I scarce turn
To view the counterfeits, the pseudo-real,
The formal flames without the fire to burn.
Love has cried yes too often. Now my ears
Are armoured to the echo, and I smile
To see the lovely boy forget his fears
And play the Trojan hero for a while.
For life has made me strong, and I resist
The fixed and fatal fancies that arise.
Enough, he said he loved me and we kissed,
To ask for more would lessen Paradise.
And yet what was potential always plods
Beside me like a herald from the gods.

Crows fly out of her skull
And the bell tolls twice,
For a world that is dull
Even in vice;
Where the pulse is blocked
By a butterfly,
And the grave has knocked
All sex awry.

To disintegrate
Through the rub of time,
And not from hate
Of an ethical line;
Proved her pelvic curve
Strict anatomy
To the untraced nerve
Of divinity.

Coral leaves embrace the green,
Skies exchange their blue.
Every summer I have seen
Keeps this rendez-vous.

But I who held high summer's rose,
Close against my heart,
Find my autumn only shows
Seasons fall apart.

From the moment we first kissed,
You became my Eucharist.

When with time I grew more wise,
You became my Paradise.

And when I die your love will be
Part of my Eternity.

This daisy-chain that does not break,
Although its petals fold for sleep.
This filament that takes the ache
Of promises we can not keep.
This cruel compartment of the heart
That no one else may occupy,
Have proved the powers of Cupid's dart
To damage and identify.

This rose embedded in the snow,
That flowers every time we meet.
This wine whose bouquet seems to grow
Until it's honeysuckle sweet.
This tide that draws us to a sea
More designate than any shore,
Are symbols of a victory
That we acknowledge and ignore.

SPANISH GRACE

Was it the way you held your head,
Proffered your hand -
Or was it an effulgence from
Your native land?

Was it contained in mobile thoughts
That found your face -
Or was it the sheer flower of
Your Spanish race?

Was it enmeshed in living flesh,
The breathing man -
Or was its source the centuries
Ere you began?

CHRYSANTHEMUMS AT CHRISTMAS

The fringes of this flower are your lips,
And in its pungent sweetness I detect
The incense of a passion in eclipse
Between the actual and the retrospect.
The coldness of this flower has a calm
As pure and perfect as the one I knew
When love deliberately exchanged the balm
Of honied entrance in a kiss that grew
Into the mutual moment that remains
Tied to the time and yet forever free,
A memory that pleases while it pains,
A fact with all a fable's poetry,
And which I seek again in this rich bloom
Amidst the censure of an empty room.

You made the daffodils seem pinchbeck gold
And dimmed the crocus' petals into dun,
Against you, the laburnum's glow was cold
And fickle Day preferred you to the Sun.
The primrose paled to snow when you were near
And buttercups were blanched beside your tread,
The topaz drained its lustre in a tear
And marigolds formed chaplets for the dead.
For you are all the gold of all the world
My bright Apollo who out-vies the Sun,
In vain are nature's colours now unfurled
When their entirety's contained in one
Sweet Alchemist, whose passion can transmute
Love's silver flower to its golden fruit.

FOR MEGAN, ON THE DEATH OF HER MOTHER

I trace the pain apparent in your face
That maps the fearful anguish that you knew
When the austerity of final grace
Became the indication life was through.

I watch the ragged banner of your mouth
Torn by the endless conflict of a mind
That sees the cancelled gardens of the south
Beside the wilderness that's left behind.

Though nothing can restore the treasured breath,
Remember, when you see the empty glove -
Against the fierce finality of death
She left the actuality of love.

TO SHAKESPEARE - ON READING HIM AT RANDOM

This time, once more, I find a further jewel
In that close cluster that we call your crown.
A crystal whose refulgence would be cruel,
But for the height from which it splinters down.
This time, again, I marvel quite anew
At ecstasy and excellence combined,
At words whose sound and rhythm are so true
They act the passion that they have designed.
Oh, Emperor of Language, such a gift
As you have given makes the world seem small,
For you can mirror nature and then shift
From physical to mental to enthral:
And flesh and spirit fuse within a line
That forges feeling for succeeding time.

SHAKESPEARE

So sweet was ne'er so fatal, for his skill
Presumes his heart and blood and makes me long
To hold a hand I know I never will,
Although my mind is fainting from his song.
So sweet was ne'er so fatal, for the past
Has pulled me from the present and I stay
Delivered to a joy that holds me fast,
And caught in a most passionate dismay:
For he both is, and is not, and this state,
So wasteful, yet so wonderful, is sad,
For phantom flesh can never correlate
With ecstasy I know, but never had.
Three hundred years divide me from my king,
"And night-owls shriek where mounting larks should sing."

ON SEEING THE DROESHOUT ENGRAVING
IN THE FIRST FOLIO

This picture has appeared a thousand times,
And I have looked at it with fond regard,
Its features as symmetric as his rhymes,
Its countenance symbolic of the Bard.
This etching almost seemed a second crest,
A formal tribute to his matchless mind,
Until in the First Folio I possessed
The actual Shakespeare Droeshout had designed.
And suddenly the wooden face caught life
And pulsed before me with poetic fire,
I saw the tenderness become the strife
Of Shakespeare vulnerable in his desire.
And in a swift affinity of pain
I felt his sorrow seek my soul again.

I thought the trees would lose their leaves
Although it was but May,
I thought the birds would cease to sing
On such a bitter day;
I thought the sun would hide his head
Amidst the darkest cloud,
I thought my sorrow was so deep
The world would cry aloud.

I thought the tide no more would turn
Obedient to the moon,
I thought the day would never end
Or sleep refuse its boon;
I thought a blight would come with night
And ruin every flower,
I thought my heart would stay its beat
In such a bitter hour.

But life went on just as before
With sun and leaves and birds,
The tide came in and then went out
Despite your bitter words;
A solemn lesson I have learned,
A strange and wondrous thing -
That hearts can break and still beat on,
That agony can sing.

The savage tortures of the Inquisition,
The beating, boiling, burning, rack and screw,
The even fiercer means to thwart perdition,
Are torments of an age I never knew.
The whipping-post, the hurdle and the brand,
The throbbing temple forced against the gun,
The turning tide, to those immersed in sand,
Are studs upon a gauntlet I've not run.
And yet the pangs involved in loving you
Would need a double Dante to expound,
The ambivalence that I'm subjected to
Is proof how sorely love and fear are bound.
Oh merciless mechanics of the heart
That make me stop what I most long to start.

My mind said love was over, and I closed
The open book of memories you left,
The past was past, and I was not disposed
To have a heart so permanently cleft.
I knew time was a healer and I felt
The axiom would prove its truth to me,
And though my wayward heart would sometimes melt
In retrospect surrender, I was free.
For life appeared a garden and the rose
Was only one of many flowers there,
I had no separate reason to suppose
The rose would still remain beyond compare,
But when I thought the force of love was spent,
I found the god was still omnipotent!

Send my boughs leafless to the summer sky,
As perquisite of that sweet-fevered June
That made the very sap of love run dry,
And left all other summers set in gloom.
Or promise me a winter that will kill
Spring's unrequired buds within my heart,
Or look on me with loathing, and so chill
The inadvertent fires that you start.
Snuff out the sun or bleach the heaven's blue,
Take measures superhuman, so they bring
An end to this outrageous love of you,
This too-abundant, futile flowering.
And yet, with you for root, what can there be,
But blossom after blossom on the tree?

All the pale winter
I bravely forgot him,
Whirled with the snowflakes,
Danced with the rain;
But now that it's April
The strong sun has brought him,
Lancing my laughter,
Piercing my pain.
No orchard in blossom
But stabs with its beauty,
Birds' sweet crescendos
Answer my sighs,
Though I sink to the dark
Gentle earth to renew me,
The blue arched above me
Looks down with his eyes.

S O N N E T

"Nothing for them was shapen but to sunder."

Old Spanish ballad.

"Nothing for them was shapen but to sunder,"
A poet wrote of lovers long ago,
And yet today this line brings little wonder
To those who understand such words of woe.
To those who have beheld the holy flower
And felt the benediction of its dew,
And triumphed in their passion's perfect hour,
And known their very being born anew:
Only to find a cruel Fate was waiting
To disallow the joys that sought to grow,
To castigate the hope still hesitating,
To confiscate what memory could bestow,
To separate the sinews of the heart
And make a space for misery to start.

For Corky

You are not two
And yet I see
Such shoots of
Femininity,
I by-pass time
To precompose
The final structure
Of the rose.

You are not two,
And yet your face
Is set with such
Enduring grace,
That passing years
Will only yield
Triumphant lilies
Of the field.

You are not two,
And we are blessed
To see potential
Loveliness,
For childhood days
Too soon depart,
Oh small infanta
Of our heart.

FOR DAVID'S MOTHER

In this hard waiting
With every nerve oppressed,
Night is a darkness
That cannot give you rest.
In this long vigil
That often seems unreal,
Truth is more savage
Than anything you feel.

And there are moments
When love seems to be
Tears in the prism
Of agony.
For every hour
Strikes with the pain
That no skill can make him
Conscious again.

But grief has limits
And time's long hand
Will lead you from the sorrow
His illness spanned,
And you will remember
The rose of his breath,
Instead of the flower
Drifting to death.

Before you came, a tree remained a tree,
Its beauty was intrinsic, though it spread
Its long green arms in glory over me,
A diadem of leaves above my head.
Until you spoke, the lilac stayed a flower,
A purple tassel waving to the Spring,
I did not know that Love possessed the power
To pierce my heart with such a fragile thing.
But since your kiss all beauty's charged with pain,
Evocative of actions now long past,
Of passion fused with passion, yet in vain,
Of ecstasy that wasn't meant to last.
These are the wounds of love you left with me,
Stigmata of the heart that none can see.

And does it end like this, quite, quite alone,
The island Donne denied most surely there,
And fractured hope that time can not postpone,
All bridges broken and the landscape bare?
And does it end like this, with memory's store
A perjured rose and echoes of a sigh,
And all the promised paths that were no more
Than terraces to castles-in-the-sky?
By loss or by desertion we are left
Without the unity of former ways,
The past annulled, the future quite bereft,
Alone within the prison of our days.
Apart, we watch life's pageantry pass by,
The shadow-people queuing up to die.

Wrapped in the strong bark of the winter trees
The buds are safe,
Theirs is a sanctuary no frost can freeze,
No winds can chafe.

Stark in the earth the silent roots will hold
The tempest's strain,
Although the branches cry against the bold
Curt hurricane.

Safely delivered to the spring will be
A flower fair,
Achievement of the utmost constancy,
Profuse and rare.

In the receding shadow of things past,
Of things long dead and gently in the grave,
My memory seeks in vain for what will last
Into the sunlight of my present age.
Fleet childhood ghosts escape my firmest hold,
And dear-loved friends resist my fiercest power
To bring them back to life, though I make bold
To try the very door of Death's dark tower.
But you, sweet love, come though I beg you not,
Appear so vividly, I stretch my hand
To take your own - then, passion overwrought,
Let fall my robe and loose my soul's last band
To nothing but the air. I pray you, stay
An ocean and three thousand miles away.

Death could not last long enough for me:
Though Shakespeare prophesied a dateless night,
My sorrow seeks a new eternity
With darkness so inimical to light,
That galaxies of suns could not conspire
To permeate the surface of its gloom,
And Christ's whole heart, that flaming rose of fire,
Could not suffuse the darkness of the tomb.
And to this darkness I would add a chill,
A curling coldness that was so profound,
The deepest nerve of life would yet lie still,
However sweet the miracle it found,
And when Jehovah cried - "Let there be light!"
My soul would still be sealed in endless night.

SONNET FOR ENGLAND

All trees are lovely, but these English trees
Are lovelier than any trees I know,
Whether their tender leaves entice the breeze,
Or their rich branches tempt the falling snow.
All trees are lovely, but these trees we love
Are conscious of the chordae of our heart,
Their tension takes our passion like a dove,
Their branches mourn that life and leaves depart.
But these proud trees have still a prouder claim,
They stand forever in our country's art,
Bare ruined choirs evermore the same,
And canvas beauty seasons cannot part.
For Shakespeare's lines engraved his native land,
And Constable held England in his hand.

MILLENNIAL SONNET

A thousand years this village on the hill
Has felt the tread of feet, the touch of hands,
It has renewed itself beneath the will
Of those who ploughed and planned its ancient lands:
Proud of its age, which Ethelred confirms,
Proud of its beauty, which the Heath sustains,
Proud of its buildings, which have come to terms
Blending the new to please more distant claims.
Hampstead the home of artists, those who sought
To catch with pen or palette what life meant,
Hampstead the home of Keats, whose genius brought
Fame, like a wayward girl, to rest content.
Hampstead whose past and present prove today
The binding intricate of England's way.

INDEX OF FIRST LINES